What people are saying about this book...

Ron Duncan is a leader whose walk matches his talk. His passionate love for the Scriptures not only shines though on every page of this book, but it shows up in every aspect of his life.

Every serious disciple of Christ should read *The Life-Changing Power of God's Word*. It will refresh, illuminate, encourage, and challenge any believer to dig deeper into the Word of God.

> Dr. Stan Toler, Author and
> General Superintendent
> Church of the Nazarene
> Oklahoma City, Oklahoma

Dr. Ron Duncan has given us a road map for renewal and unity by applying the transforming power of God's Word. It is a simple, practical, and powerful book that comes from the heart and speaks to the heart. It reveals his passion for the church, his loyalty to and faith in the Word of God, and his dependence on the wisdom and enablement of the Holy Spirit.

I wholeheartedly endorse *The Life-Changing Power of God's Word*. It points the church toward spiritual renewal and unity; and it should be put in the hands of every pastor, church leader, and disciple who longs to be true to the Master and biblical truth.

> Dr. Bill C. Konstantopoulos
> Author and Evangelist
> Johnson City, Tennessee

Dr. Ronald Duncan has captured in this book a vital fact that is often lost in a world that is overwhelmed with facts: God's Word is able to change people, congregations, and even nations. Dr. Duncan sums up this very thought when he says that God "did it in the first century, and he can do it again today."

As Dr. Duncan walks through some of these wonderful truths of God, he shares his personal accounts of many years of ministry and life. So it is an intensely personal account.

If you are serious about seeing your life changed by the Word of God, I encourage you to read this book.

Pastor H. Gerald Rudd
Greeneville, Tennessee

This book is enjoyable and profitable to read, full of practical insights for effective Christian living. Ron addresses the challenges facing the church with a joyous confidence built upon the solid rock of the Word of God. Each chapter is built upon a passage of Scripture and is re-readable as a devotional or as the source for group or individual study.

Ron's desire to see Christians filled with the Holy Spirit and the church operating as God's chief transformation agent in this world, is both tangible and irresistible. The power and practicality of the Word of God is brought before us, sprinkled with love, humility, and refreshing humor. Ron presents the lessons of a lifetime spent in the trenches of Christian service and makes them easily accessible to the reader.

I heartily recommend this book! You will be blessed as Ron instructs and invites you to "make God's promises your window on the world."

Rev. Charles Myricks Jr.
Chief Operating and Development Officer
National Association of the Church of God

The Life-Changing
Power of God's Word

The Life-Changing Power of God's Word

Studies in the Book of Romans

By Ronald V. Duncan

Warner Press
Anderson, Indiana

Coordinator of Publishing & Creative Services
Church of God Ministries, Inc.
PO Box 2420
Anderson, IN 46018-2420
800-848-2464
www.chog.org

To purchase additional copies of this book, to inquire about distribution, and for all other sales-related matters, please contact:

Warner Press, Inc.
PO Box 2499
Anderson, IN 46018-2499
800-741-7721
www.warnerpress.org

ISBN: 978-1-59317-581-8

Printed in the United States of America.

12 13 14 15 16 17 / TPS / 10 9 8 7 6 5 4 3 2 1

Contents

Foreword ix

Introduction. 1

1. A New Command 5

2. Being the Body of Christ 15

3. The Gospel in Your Life 25

4. Unwavering Faith. 35

5. Grace for Difficult Questions 43

6. Placed in the Body of Christ. 53

7. Holy Spirit 101. 61

8. The Power of Divine Love 71

9. Accountable for Spiritual Growth 81

10. Hope for the Future 89

A Final Word 97

Foreword

The inspiration for a book emerges from numerous sources. This book is the result of a speaking assignment at White Hall Camp Meeting in August 2011, and I am thankful to the leaders of Western Pennsylvania for that opportunity. I am also grateful for the urging of Joe Allison to compile those messages in a book and for his support in editing it, along with Stephen Lewis. (A free study guide has also been created for this book and is available online at http://alturl.com/6u5gv.)

Let me make a brief comment about the context of this book. The vision and mission statement of the Church of God movement is, "Transforming Culture by Being the Body of Christ." That statement was proposed by the Strategic Planning Conference in 2006 and endorsed by the Ministries Council and the 2007 General Assembly. However, it was a guiding principle of my ministry long before that. It is my firm belief that the Christian faith demonstrated by believers, in and through the life of the church, can change our culture for God's glory. Our culture has been heavily influenced by secular humanism, and Christians must do everything possible to swing the pendulum back toward the Judeo-Christian ethic that laid the foundation of Western civilization.

In order for the church to transform our culture, we must renew our focus on the life-changing power of the Word of God. Therefore, my goal in these chapters is to present several contemporary issues that are addressed by the powerful Word of the Lord. Obviously, I will not attempt to cover every issue before us. However, I trust that this inquiry will inspire change within the moral fabric of individual Christians so that the collective body, the church, will influence our society as God intends.

Ron Duncan
April 2012

Introduction

I have had numerous conversations with individuals from all walks of life concerning the role and impact of the Bible in daily living. For many in our culture, the Bible is a book, a book that might be referenced at some point, but certainly not central to the thinking process that sets up core values and parameters for living. Some see the Bible as irrelevant literature, outdated, with stories that are difficult to understand and apply with certainty in our era. Even Christians have differences about the role of the Bible.

As believers in Jesus Christ, we have a decision to make concerning the role and impact we allow the Word of God to have in our lives. Believers generally fall into three categories when it comes to their use of the Bible: Surface, Pick and Choose, and Integrated. For those in the Surface category, the Word of God has very little impact on how they function; it is used whenever it is convenient and needed. Believers in the Pick and Choose category use the Word of God to prove whatever they desire. Integrated believers see the Word of God as integral to life development, interpret it with a sound process and studies, and learn and meditate on its truths.

As a believer and disciple of the Lord Jesus Christ, I strive to integrate the Word of God into my decision-making and lifestyle. The writer of Hebrews says, "Indeed, the word of God is living and active, sharper than any two-edged sword, piercing until it divides soul from spirit, joints from marrow; it is able to judge the thoughts and intentions of the heart"(4:12). Paul instructed young Timothy, "All scripture is inspired by God and is useful for teaching, for reproof, for correction, and for training in righteousness, so that everyone who belongs to God may be proficient, equipped for every good work."(2 Tim 3:16–17).

Just from these two texts it is clear that Scripture should be powerful, transforming our lives. If Scripture is not performing this function in our lives, why is it not? I have identified several causes.

The first reason is laziness. Reading the Bible takes a certain amount of discipline. When a person becomes a Christian, accepting Christ as Lord and Savior, he or she is most likely to practice the same pattern of study he or she used before becoming a Christian. In our culture today, most people rely on constant external stimuli (e.g., television, radio, Twitter, Facebook) for information. Reading a book simply is not fast enough, especially if they have to learn how to read the book.

The second reason is overload. Information abounds in the world today. We simply cannot keep up with the information explosion. Most of us are on overload. Furthermore, the quality and importance of the data are not apparent, causing some people to shut down. As a result, we hear statements like, "I am going to stick with simple"; "I know what I believe and that's enough"; "Let the experts figure it out."

The third reason is confusion. When new believers hear various interpretations of a particular text, they develop questions about the validity of the Bible. If certain parts can be interpreted differently by the experts, then what chance do I have in understanding and more importantly getting answers to my questions?

The fourth reason is inoculation. Some believers get just enough Scripture in the beginning to be inoculated from the real significance of the Bible. You remember how it goes: The new believer is given certain scriptures to memorize. The purpose of the memorization is to ground them in the faith. Once this task is complete, many feel they are done, when in reality they are just beginning.

So if we want Scripture to transform the lives of believers, how can we teach, train, disciple, and model in such a way that this happens? The answer is found in the opposite of the reasons just listed: discipline, not laziness; selective data input to avoid overload; hermeneutics instead of confusion; and immersion in the Word rather than inoculation.

All of us need help. We need help to move from the place where we are to another place, one where we will stay for a while before moving forward again. The Christian faith is a journey. The destination, someone has said, is the journey. The place we find ourselves today is for today, but maybe not for tomorrow. In order for Scripture to continue to make a difference in our lives, we must continue to move forward. Previous generations would have said that we need to "keep walking in the light as the light is revealed."

I have a theory about maturation and growth that I have tested by observing hundreds of people. It seems rather clear to me that growth and maturation occur when what is known is integrated into life values, preparing the way for additional growth and maturation. This means an individual incorporates a value into life, which then guides a behavior and lifestyle. When conflicting values exist (the old way with the new way), the individual is stymied until this conflict is resolved. Growth and maturation come to a halt. The key to growth is resolution of the conflict. It is very difficult, if not impossible, to grow and mature while entertaining conflicting values.

As an example, consider newborn Christians trying to follow Christ faithfully while dealing with their old ways of living. This growth process never stops, but one must seek to find harmony among the values he or she holds. Once an individual embraces a value consistent with biblical holiness, it is essential for actions to flow from this value. At first the new Christian may take two steps forward and one step back, but the power of the Holy Spirit assists the believer in achieving consistency with the new belief system and the behaviors.

Most of us like it when what we are learning can be applied readily to our lives and when we see the difference it makes. I contend that Scripture should be making a difference in the way we live. The application may be immediate or it may take a while, but the end result should be viewable.

In order for Scripture to have its greatest impact on our lives, I see several essential steps. Step one is for the individual to reach a point in his or her life experience with a full acknowledgement of this fact: I need the power of God and his understanding in my life in order to survive and thrive. This is a realization that God is and must be involved in my daily experience.

Step two is a commitment to the Bible as the Word of God and a learning attitude toward it. The Bible is truly unique. You and I can both read it, understand it, and be inspired by it in different ways. The Bible is our source for values that guide and determine our behaviors. God breathed life into humanity when he started with Adam. God gives abundant life on earth and eternal life in heaven for the believer. The believer's task is to attempt to master the resources God has provided for the believer, starting with the Bible. The lack of Bible literacy is at the core of the problem of anemic churches and apathetic Christians. The average Christian in America has an inconsistent Bible-reading plan and a hodgepodge of beliefs based on cultural values, family values, and tradition. The lack of a well-grounded, systemic biblical worldview breeds difficulties and troubles of all sorts for the individual and the church. Basic biblical knowledge is essential in order for the believer to enthusiastically engage in a faithful journey.

Step three is participation in a community of believers. I define *community* as any person or group of persons that provides a safe learning atmosphere for the believer. Community can be and should be a church family, but it is not limited to church family. Each person must have some place to ask questions, share frustrations, and wander around while searching for answers. Many have the mistaken idea that everyone else has it figured out and that they are the only ones still working at a solution. In reality, most have arrived at the starting point and have started the journey with some success, but no one has arrived. Remember, the destination is the journey.

So these three steps—recognition of need, commitment to the Bible, and community—are vital components as we seek to allow the Bible to transform our lives.

My intention in this book is to provide numerous examples of the transforming power of Scripture on subjects that are at the core of our faith.

Chapter 1

A New Command

I give you a new commandment, that you love one another. Just as I have loved you, you also should love one another. By this everyone will know that you are my disciples, if you have love for one another. —John 13:34–35

The Word of God is powerful. It can change the lives of individuals, heal broken marriages, revitalize congregations, and transform the cultures of great empires. In the pages that follow, we will consider some of the most transformative passages of Scripture. As we do, I challenge you to apply God's Word to your own life. Hebrews 4:12 tells us that "the word of God is living and active, sharper than any two-edged sword, piercing until it divides soul from spirit, joints from marrow; it is able to judge the thoughts and intentions of the heart." May this study of God's Word change your life in such a radical way.

We begin with a word from our Lord Jesus Christ. To grasp the full import of this word, we need to consider its context.

If you had only had a few hours to live, what would you tell your friends, family, and co-workers? Let's say you call your closest friends together to tell them something that will change their lives. What would you say? What would you want them to hear from your dying lips?

That's the context of this passage from John 13. The night before he was crucified, Jesus had called his disciples together in an upper room to share a Passover meal. There he washed their feet—which amazed them—and then he said, "I give you a new commandment."

I served in the United States Army for twenty-five years, so I know what a command is. A command means, "You do this." Without dispute, without hesitation, with your whole heart. So what does Jesus command his disciples to do? "Love one another."

When you first read that, you may scratch your head and say, "Really? This is a 'new command'? Haven't these men loved each other for three years? Sure, they might bicker among themselves sometimes, and they didn't always put the other disciples' needs ahead of their own. But they lived together and traveled together 24/7. Surely they loved each other."

Here's the catch. In this most critical moment of their life together, Jesus tells the Twelve, "I'm giving you a new command. I want you to love one another as I have loved you." That's pretty simple, isn't it?

Not really. I've seen so many congregations that are dysfunctional, congregations in which the people do not love each other as Christ did. Take a candid look at your own congregation and ask, "Are we acting like Christ? Are we living as Christ lived and loving one another as he loves us?" You see, Christians are called to live according to the Word of God. If our behavior differs from what the Word says, then we had better change our behavior. And here's Jesus' final word to his followers: "Just as I have loved you, you also should love one another."

When I was a boy, my mother used switches to punish me. Those green, sappy branches would sting my bare legs in a most convincing way. So if I misbehaved, she'd say, "Go get me a switch." I would find the smallest branch I could—yet she somehow made it work! One day, I came back without anything. "Well," she said, "where is my switch?"

"Mom, we're out of them," I said.

Seriously, despite all the bushes that grew in our front yard, the good switches were gone because she had needed so many. My behavior did not match her commands.

When Christians' behavior falls short of the Lord's commands, we have dysfunction in the life of the church. When a congregation is no longer motivated by divine love, the results can be painful, even disastrous.

Jesus' kind of love comes only from the Holy Spirit. When Jesus commanded the Twelve to love one another with the same kind of agape love he had shown them, he knew the Holy Spirit would soon come upon them and they would receive this gift. That's what John 13 says. Let's look more closely at what happens when we have that kind of love.

The infilling of the Holy Spirit bathes our attitudes and dispositions in the love of God. Jesus described this in his high priestly prayer, recorded in John 17:

> "As you, Father, are in me and I am in you, may they also be in us, so that the world may believe that you have sent me. The glory that you have given me I have given them, so that they may be one, as we are one, I in them and you in me, that they may become completely one, so that the world may know that you have sent me and have loved them even as you have loved me. Father, I desire that those also, whom you have given me, may be with me where I am, to see my glory, which you have given me because you loved me before the foundation of the world.
>
> "Righteous Father, the world does not know you, but I know you; and these know that you have sent me. I made your name known to them, and I will make it known, so that the love with which you have loved me may be in them, and I in them." (John 17:21b–26)

Think of a tense relationship in your neighborhood or the place where you work. Ask yourself, Is divine love being lived there? If you are the pastor of a church, are you loving all of your board members? Are you loving everyone who is in a position of leadership in your congregation? Do you really love them, or are you just tolerating them. (There's a difference, and people know it.)

Martha and I are fortunate to have three children and, currently, eight grandchildren. Those grandchildren know that we love them, and because we do, we want to see them grow and mature. We want the best for them.

Now look at the life of your local church. Do you want the best for everybody there? Does everybody in your congregation want the best for each other, no matter whether they get their own way?

I wish I could say that was true everywhere, but it's not. So we have to ask, "How are we going to make a difference in the lives of other people unless we love each other with unconditional agape love? Jesus said, "By this everyone will know that you are my disciples, if you have love for one another."

Receive the Holy Spirit

Since agape love is given to us by the Holy Spirit and that gift has the power to elevate us to a relationship that mirrors the love Jesus Christ has for his disciples, one question remains: Have you received the Holy Spirit? This is the first challenge I give you: Receive the Holy Spirit in all of his fullness.

As the apostle Paul went to Ephesus, he came upon a group of people who had been converted. He asked them this question: "Have you received the Holy Spirit?"

They said, "We have never heard of such a thing."

So Paul instructed them. Then the text says they received the Holy Spirit and great and wonderful things began to happen in the life of the Ephesian church (Acts 19:1ff). I believe many congregations today are spiritually anemic because they are not filled with the Holy Spirit, who would give them the ability to love one another as well as their surrounding community.

George Barna, Reggie McNeil, and a host of other observers say that today's church is inept and weak, so it is unable to affect our secular culture. It is clear that in order to do what Jesus commanded us to do, we need to be filled with the Holy Spirit.

For several decades, we've had a bit of confusion about the work of the Holy Spirit. I grew up in east Tennessee, not far from Cleveland, Tennessee. Cleveland is the home of the neo-Pentecostal denomination known as the Church of God (the other Church of God, we called it). We also had other Church of God folks who handled poisonous snakes. So our congregation in Kingsport always made a distinction. "We're not those folks," we would say. Nonetheless we expected and sought the infilling of the Holy Spirit.

When I was a pastor in Pasadena, Texas, a woman called me and asked, "Do you believe in the *charismata*?"

I knew that *charismata* was the Greek New Testament word for the gifts of the Spirit, so I said, "Of course, we do."

"Do you practice them?"

I said, "Absolutely."

"Then I'll be at your church on Sunday."

She did attend our worship service that Sunday, and at the end of the service I went out to greet people. When she came by, she said, "You lied to me."

"What do you mean?" I asked.

"Nobody in this service spoke in tongues," she said.

"I didn't say that we spoke in tongues," I replied. "You asked if we practice the *charismata*, the gifts of the Spirit, and we do. There are twenty-seven of them in the New Testament and I think we practiced twenty-six of them this week."

She stormed out.

That's just one example of people's confusion about the role of the Holy Spirit. Some think the infilling of the Holy Spirit is a one-time experience. If you receive the fullness of the Spirit, they believe you don't need to receive any more. Others say, no, a believer continues to receive more of the Spirit's fullness as you need him, because you're going to grow. That's what I believe. Throughout the New Testament, we see the Holy Spirit evidenced in the lives of God's people, but his infilling is not as a static experience. We need to have the Holy Spirit's power refreshed within us, day after day.

I've been involved in ministry for more than forty-six years, and I can tell you that not every Christian is spiritually mature. We have baby Christians who get started in a life of faith but never grow up spiritually. When we accept Jesus Christ as our Savior and Lord, we begin a journey of spiritual growth. Read what happened to the apostle Paul; if he wasn't growing spiritually throughout his whole ministry, I don't know who was. Look at the apostle Peter and the change in his understanding of God's purpose for the Gentiles. Look at the growth that happened to the entire church in the book of Acts.

Let's be honest. If you have never prayed, "Lord, fill me with your Spirit," you need to grow up. You need to take the next step of faith and keep moving forward in Christ every day. Otherwise, you will be a spiritual infant all of your life.

Be Reconciled

Secondly, I challenge you to resolve any dispute that you have with another believer. Allow no grudges to divide the body of Christ. In Matthew 5, Jesus says, "When you are offering your gift at the altar, if you remember that your brother or sister has something against you, leave your gift there before the altar and go; first be reconciled to your brother or sister, and then come and offer your gift" (vv 23–24). This kind of forgiveness is a sign of spiritual maturity, and it is possible only when the Holy Spirit controls us. When someone feels slighted or offended by something we've done, our carnal nature says, "Let them come to me; it's their problem." But the Holy Spirit moves us to go to them and seek reconciliation so that nothing separates us from one another in the body of Christ.

If the Holy Spirit convicts you of the need to be reconciled with another Christian, be glad. You are in a good place, not a bad place.

Be Healed

The third challenge I give you is to seek the Holy Spirit's healing for any personal need you have. Whether it is a physical ailment or a deep emotional scar, the Holy Spirit can soothe and encourage you. He will never turn you away. We read in the epistle of James:

> Are any among you sick? They should call for the elders of the church and have them pray over them, anointing them with oil in the name of the Lord. The prayer of faith will save the sick, and the Lord will raise them up; and anyone who has committed sins will be forgiven. Therefore confess your sins to one another, and pray for one another, so that you may be healed. The prayer of the righteous is powerful and effective. (James 5:14–16)

Some years ago, I was called to the residence of a daughter of one of our beloved and elderly saints. The daughter told me that she believed her elderly mother was dying. It was extremely difficult for her to get out of bed and get around. She had told her daughter, "Call our pastor so he can pray for my healing." I was a relatively young pastor at that time. Having arrived at the residence, the daughter instructed me to accompany her into the bedroom to see her mother. The light was dim and her mother seemed to be breathing heavily. I called her name and touched her hand as I sat down next to the bed. She responded with gracious words and thanked me for coming. After talking for a few minutes, I shared some scripture, anointed her head with oil, and prayed a prayer of faith for her physical healing. As I left, she gripped my hand and once again thanked me for coming. As we came to the kitchen, the daughter asked if I would like a cup of coffee and fresh apple pie. While we were eating and talking, the door to the bedroom opened and out walked her mother. She came to the table and said, "I would like some pie also." As a young pastor, I sat there thrilled, amazed, and grateful. Her mother lived several more years, and when she died, I conducted her funeral. I know without a doubt that the Holy Spirit of God touched her body that day; I was simply the instrument for the moment. As dynamic and powerful as physical healing may be, I believe greater healings come through the Holy Spirit when scarred minds and hearts are renewed and revitalized.

Divorce in our culture is rampant and, in most instances, very destructive. Who is right and who is wrong in the relationship loses its significance as the years pass. Yet the anger and unforgiveness that abide in the hearts and minds of all involved continue to influence lives and decisions daily. An individual who has been hurt in this manner finds it extremely difficult, if not impossible, to forgive. The animosity and distrust of the other person seem to grow like unwanted weeds until all that is seen are the weeds. I have conducted hundreds of counseling sessions with persons contemplating or experiencing divorce, knowing that they will be maimed for life unless they are filled with God's Holy Spirit, which will provide them the power to have agape love and to forgive.

I believe the reason the church is experiencing so much dysfunction today is because the Christians within the church have failed to realize the need to be filled with the Holy Spirit so that they can love as Jesus loves. The disciples would not have been able to love as Jesus loves without the infilling of the Holy Spirit. They would not have had the courage to go forward, speak boldly, and take on both the religious and secular worlds they were facing without the Holy Spirit.

This text is just one of the promises of healing that we find in God's Word, and there are many more. In both the Old and New Testaments, the Bible assures us that God is eager to bring wholeness and health to all of his children.

The Word of God

These are just a few of the life-changing words that we find in Scripture, and I will invite you to apply several others to your life in the chapters to come. People take one of three basic positions with respect to God's Word, and your position will determine whether the Word changes your life.

The first position is *fascination*. If you are fascinated with Scripture, you examine it and ponder its beauty, but you never apply it to your own life. You treat Scripture like a museum relic. "Oh, that sounds good," you say, "but I'm just not sure about it."

The second position is *skepticism*. You hear Scripture in worship services and discussion groups, you may even read the Bible devotionally now and then, but you don't believe it really is God's Word. You play along with other people who respect it. You say to yourself, "The Bible? It's for those religious types, but it doesn't really apply to me."

The third position is *faith*. You trust that God inspired godly people to write the Bible, and you believe with 2 Timothy 3:16 that God uses the Bible to guide, comfort, and admonish his people in every generation. So you say, "The Bible is true for all humanity, and it's true for me. This is the truth by which I must live." This is my position, and I pray that it's yours as well. I believe that if we receive Scripture by faith as the Word of God, then God will use it to change our lives.

When we read the Scriptures together at our home church each week, our worship leader concludes the reading with a simple yet powerful statement of faith. I invite you to say it as your own affirmation of faith every time you read the Bible:

The Word of God,
for the people of God!
Thanks be to God!

Chapter 2

Being the Body of Christ

I appeal to you therefore, brothers and sisters, by the mercies of God, to present your bodies as a living sacrifice, holy and acceptable to God, which is your spiritual worship. Do not be conformed to this world, but be transformed by the renewing of your minds, so that you may discern what is the will of God—what is good and acceptable and perfect. —Romans 12:1–2

The only way we will make a difference in today's world is to begin acting like the church described in the New Testament. Even though it was small and struggling, the early church made a tremendous difference in the culture of which it was a part. We too will make a difference if we embody the values of the New Testament church. What are those values?

At a Strategic Planning Conference in Nashville, Tennessee, in 2006, the 146 leaders of the Church of God (Anderson, Indiana) who had gathered from around the country adopted the following vision and mission statement:

> *Transforming the culture* [that's our vision] *by being the body of Christ* [that's our mission].

In addition, these leaders identified five strategic values that characterized the New Testament church and that should be true of the church today. The strategic values are as follows:

The Great Commission

The first strategic value of the church is *revitalizing the Great Commission*. In Matthew 28, Jesus says, "Go and make disciples." That is a command. That is an imperative. That is the Great Commission, which Jesus gave to all of his disciples. That commission belongs to us two thousand years later. Christ expects us to be going and making disciples for him. This is a basic task of the New Testament church.

If you are a football enthusiast, you know the importance of practicing the basics of the game. Every football coach makes this point in locker-room speeches to his team: "We need to practice the basics—blocking and tackling." If a football team does not do that, they will lose the game. Tony Dungy, former coach of the Indianapolis Colts, spoke at a citywide worship service in my hometown a couple of years ago. He said, "No matter the talents of my players, no matter how good they are, no matter their physical condition, no matter how much they know, until they do the basics together, they are not a team."

What does that say about the life of the church? Until we practice the New Testament basics together, we're not Christ's team and we cannot accomplish the mission he has given us.

When I was about age fifteen, my local congregation was erecting a new building. The people came together and contributed what they had to help raise that building. Some were carpenters, some were masons, some were electricians, and some were just go-fers like me. But we all came together in order to get the job done. That's the only way we can fulfill the Great Commission. Did Jesus say, "Go and make disciples," to just one-tenth of the church? Did he say it just to one-fifteenth of the church? No, he said it to every believer.

A Fuller Theological Seminary study found that it takes eighty-five people to lead one person to Christ in churches more than ten years old. Imagine that—eighty-five Christians just to make one convert. The same study found that in churches less than three years old, it takes three people to lead one person to Christ.[1] A large number of the people who live around you in a typical American neighborhood do not know Jesus Christ. For most churches, it takes contact by eighty-five Christians to bring just one of those people to Christ each year. So how are we doing, team? How's that working?

---

1. As quoted by Simple Church, "Why Simply Church?" http://www.simplechurchat home.com/Why.html.

George Barna says that almost one-half of all churches in America (there are approximately 325,000 total) do not have one convert in a year's time. Think about that: The church is the body of Christ. The church has the mission to go and make disciples for Christ. Yet one-half of American churches won't bring one person to Christ this year. Tell me, do you think the Great Commission is important to us? It isn't. Because if it were, we would be accomplishing our mission.

We in the Church of God have got to get back to the basics of being the church. And the first basic, Jesus said, is to go and make disciples.

The Greatest Commandments

The second strategic value is *engaging every disciple in the Great Commandments*. In Matthew 25:37–39, Jesus said that the greatest commandments are to love the Lord your God with all your heart, soul, and mind, and love your neighbor as yourself.

Now who is your neighbor?

All human beings belong to God, and a great many of them—far more than 40 percent—are in dire need. Art Clausen spent a year in Haiti coordinating the efforts of Church of God Ministries to rebuild homes after the devastating January 2010 earthquake. He tells me that as of late 2011, 70 percent of the people in Haiti were unemployed. The average wage for those who are employed is five dollars a day. Art found tremendous need in Haiti, and it's just one small part of our world.

Slightly more than 40 percent of the world's population survives on less than two dollars a day. Many people are hungry. Many people need clothing and shelter. So what does Jesus say to us about them? "For I was hungry and you gave me food, I was thirsty and you gave me something to drink, I was a stranger and you welcomed me, I was naked and you gave me clothing, I was sick and you took care of me, I was in prison and you visited me…just as you did it to one of the least of these who are members of my family, you did it to me" (Matt 25:35–36, 40). He is speaking the Word of God to us. And the Word of God says we must do something about the needs of the people around us.

Can we feed everybody? No, but who can we feed? Who can we clothe? Who can we visit? That's what it means to love your neighbor. You put yourself out for the sake of others. You sacrifice so that you can show them the love of Christ. The Great Commandments are not about convenience; they are about commitment. If we are going to transform the culture of today's world by being the body of Christ, then we have to help needy people and care for them more than we care for ourselves.

Stewardship

The New Testament's third strategic value for the church is *committing to stewardship principles (Matt. 6:33) leading to a flexible ministry future and the management of debt* (debt free as the goal) for every individual, church and agency. Jesus says in Matthew 6:33, "Strive first for the kingdom of God and his righteousness, and all these things will be given to you as well." He promises that God the Father will provide our material needs if we serve him. We do not have to encumber our future with debt to provide for ourselves today.

Many Christians are carrying a great deal of debt on their shoulders, debt that has them in a stranglehold. Even though they want to give financially to the work of God's kingdom, they cannot give because they are so deeply in debt. Congressional debates about rising deficits and debt ceilings illustrate how our culture has affected our thinking in this respect. We think we cannot live on what we earn, so we charge our expenses to the next generation. That's what raising the national debt ceiling is all about. We are putting today's burdens on the backs of those not yet born. It makes no sense. If we are going to make a difference in today's world, then we must change the way we handle the income and possessions that God has blessed us with.

Many people think the Church of God movement is poor, but it's not. Look at the cars being driven to your worship services on Sunday. And did you know that in 2010 two individuals on the Forbes 500 list (the five hundred richest people in the United States) were

Church of God people? I realize we still have plenty of congregations that are not rich, but there's more financial wealth in your local church that you might imagine. Financial experts estimate that over the next fifteen years, $26 trillion of financial assets will be transferred from one generation to another in the United States. Twenty-six trillion! I don't even know how to write that figure. And some of that transfer will occur within the Church of God.

We must come to grips with our own financial stewardship. How do we handle money? How are we caring for the material assets that God has entrusted to us?

The Church of God Foundation has developed some tools that can help us teach better stewardship in the life of the church, tools based on biblical principles. The fact is, many of our children have not received sound training in financial stewardship. We need to teach our people how to handle money responsibly; doing so is vital to the life and witness of the local church.

Consider this statement: *There is enough money in your congregation to do everything God wants you to do.* Do you agree with that? I do. But I believe that much of that money rests in the pockets of parishioners and not in the offering plate. You see, many Church of God people stopped tithing a long time ago. I know that's true because I read the statistics. We must recommit ourselves to sound stewardship principles and teach them unabashedly. The Bible says more about money than almost any other topic, so we should not hesitate to talk about it.

God has given us financial resources to be used for the work of his kingdom. Whatever we have really belongs to him. I'm thankful that I have been so blessed, and thankful that you have been so blessed, and I believe we are obliged to do ministry with those blessings. "From everyone to whom much has been given, much will be required; and from the one to whom much has been entrusted, even more will be demanded," Jesus says (Luke 12:48b).

Spiritual Gifts

The fourth strategic value is *nurturing the spiritual gifts* of every individual, congregation, and church agency. Several years ago,

Church of God Ministries conducted a survey of the Church of God (Anderson, Indiana) in the United States. We asked three thousand Church of God people, "Are you using your spiritual gifts in the life of the church?" The first problem we encountered was that many people did not understand what a spiritual gift is. Apparently, they had not read 1 Corinthians 12, Romans 12, or Ephesians 4, where the apostle Paul describes the gifts that God gives us so that his body can function. The gift of hospitality, the gift of mercy, the gift of giving, the gift of administration, the gift of teaching, the gift of preaching, the gift of prophecy—God gives all of those gifts to his people. Once we defined spiritual gifts, we again asked, "Are you using your gift(s) in the life of the church?" Only two out of ten respondents said they were.

Let's put that in context. Suppose you own a business and you have ten employees. All ten show up on Monday morning, but eight of them sit down and watch the other two work. How long do you think you could stay in business?

Or suppose you were a school principal. When school starts, ten teachers and three hundred students show up, but eight of the teachers look at the other two and say, "Go get 'em! We're going to watch you teach and offer constructive criticism. We're going to point out how you could do the job better." How long do you think your school would survive?

Does this sort of thing routinely happen in our public schools? No. Does it happen in our businesses? No. Does it happen in the life of the church? Yes.

I'm not trying to make you feel depressed; I'm just pointing out the facts. The facts are, we are not getting God's work done because many of God's people believe they can choose whether or not they will be actively involved.

When you were saved by the Lord Jesus Christ, he placed you in his body. That's true according to Scripture and that's what the Church of God believes. You are now part of the body of Christ, so you have certain responsibilities to the body and you are accountable to the body. That's the way the Lord designed the church. It's clear to me that if we are going to transform our culture, we have to be the genuine body of Christ. And if we are the body of Christ, we must practice the New Testament basics of winning the lost, caring for our neighbors, dealing responsibly with our money, and using our spiritual gifts in Christian service.

Christian Unity

The fifth strategic value of the church is *renewing the relational connectivity and identity* of every individual believer, congregation, and church agency. In the high-priestly prayer of Jesus, he prayed that his people would be one (John 17). This is why the Church of God teaches the unity of all believers. It's why we say we "reach our hands to every blood-washed one." That's who we are as a movement. And if that's not who you are, it's who you ought to be.

This relational connectivity with other Christians brings power to our mission because we are a part, not only of our local church, but of all congregations and all Christians who seek to build the kingdom of God. We need to proclaim our unity and practice it.

These five strategic values define who we are and how we act. Where we have neglected these New Testament practices, we need to reclaim them. How can we do that? Hebrews 12:1–3 points the way:

> Since we are surrounded by so great a cloud of witnesses, let us also lay aside every weight and the sin that clings so closely, and let us run with perseverance the race that is set before us, looking to Jesus the pioneer and perfecter of our faith, who for the sake of the joy that was set before him endured the cross, disregarding its shame, and has taken his seat at the right hand of the throne of God. Consider him who endured such hostility against himself from sinners, so that you may not grow weary or lose heart.

Here are three practical steps that each of us can take to function more effectively within the body of Christ.

First, we can recognize and rejoice in the fact that people are watching and cheering us on. My mom and dad have passed away, and my wife's mom and dad have passed away. They were great cheerleaders for us when they were on this earth, and I believe they are still cheering us on. I believe they celebrate whenever we do what God has called us to do. I believe the same is true for you. No matter where you serve, no matter what the health of your congregation is, no matter how desperate or discouraged you may feel, a lot of people are cheering for you. Saints of God are watching, applauding, and urging you to do your best as you go forward. Every one of us can take courage in that fact.

Second (and this is the hardest step), we need to discard anything that causes us to falter in following Christ. I was not much of a high-school athlete, though I toyed with the idea. Then I enlisted in the United States Army and I had to stay physically fit. I had to run. (I ran until I ran out of run!) I had to do push-ups, sit-ups, and other sorts of exercises. I learned that I did not want a lot of excess weight, because that just dragged me back. I didn't want to carry a forty-pound pack on my back when I needed to run a race. The writer of Hebrews says, "If we're going to run the race that God has marked out for us, we must discard everything that would hinder us" (Heb 12:1, author's paraphrase).

What are some of those hindrances? One of them is an ungodly attitude. You see, the Lord God saved you for a life of repentance. The Greek word for repentance is *metanoia*, which means "to turn around and go in a new direction." Some people have professed faith in Jesus Christ, but they have not turned around. They have not gone in a new direction. And they won't be able to do that until they discard their old attitudes, biases, and prejudices.

I don't know what baggage you may have to discard, but I challenge you to pray about what you must leave behind in order to be a faithful follower of Jesus Christ. Take that sack of stuff that's preventing you from winning the race and discard it. Throw it away! Because those things will keep you from living within the body of Christ.

Third, we need to fix our eyes on Jesus. Very few people have a Christ-centered worldview. When people with a Christ-centered worldview have to make a decision, they ask, "What would Jesus do?" They see everything through Christ, who is the author and perfecter of our faith.

During Dietrich Bonhoeffer's time in a Nazi prison, he prayed for his captors and those who watched him. His motivation was his faith in Christ, which could go to the darkest places and bring light. He could have fixated on the horrible conditions in which he found himself, the unethical behavior of Hitler, or a host of other wrongs, but he chose to focus on Christ. What would happen to me if Christ motivated my attitude and behavior in all my circumstances?

Have you ever stared at someone until you got embarrassed that you were? You will never be embarrassed about focusing all of your attention on Jesus. Fix your eyes clearly on him so you can run the race of life successfully and keep the faith that has been entrusted to you.

To summarize, if we are going to transform the culture where you and I live, we must be the body of Christ. In order to be the body of Christ, we need to embody these five New Testament values in all that we do: Reach the lost people of this world. Love our neighbors. Deal honestly with our money. Use the gifts God has given us. And link arms with others who are of like faith and mind.

Let me leave you with one more word from George Barna. He predicts that by 2025, less than one-third of all Americans will look to the local congregation for their spiritual guidance.[2] Unless something significant changes in the life of the church, less than one-third of all Americans will seek spiritual guidance from the church. That's not a good picture, is it?

But we have a crowd of faithful witnesses cheering us on. We know how to do the kingdom's work. And we have the Lord himself leading the way. If we keep our attention focused on him, we will transform the world instead of being conformed to it.

---

2. George Barna, *Revolution* (Wheaton, IL: Tyndale House, 2005), 49.

Chapter 3

The Gospel in Your Life

For I am not ashamed of the gospel; it is the power of God for salvation to everyone who has faith, to the Jew first and also to the Greek.

—*Romans 1:16*

If I were to give you a sheet of paper and ask you to write down the most important fact you know, what would you write? Let me ask it in a different way: What subject do you talk about when you get together with your friends? With so much information bombarding you every day, what comes to the forefront of your conversations?

We have plenty to talk about. We live in an age of knowledge. Information just keeps multiplying. Every day brings new discoveries, new insights, and new ideas for us to digest. A host of new technologies and new networking sites are designed to help us keep up with all of this knowledge, but we often feel overwhelmed by it. So what is the most important thing you think about, write about, and talk about each day?

The apostle Paul says the good news of Jesus Christ is the most important fact any of us can know. He ought to know, because his life had been completely changed by Jesus. He had gone through a life transformation so radical that he had even changed his name. Originally named Saul, he was a devout Jew who set out to persecute the church. Acts 9 says he was on the road to Damascus about that business when he had an encounter with the Lord God Almighty. Not many of us have a Damascus Road encounter with God, but we do have divine encounters, because God does whatever is necessary to confront us with the need for transformation. So Scripture says God confronted Saul with a blinding light, and Saul was converted to Christ on that road. Later, he became known as Paul.

In Galatians 1, Paul gives his testimony to the church in Galatia. He says that after he was converted, he went to Arabia for three years. (That's quite a sabbatical. I believe he had to go away so there could be a total realignment of his mind and his heart.) Then he went to Jerusalem and talked to the apostle Peter. He began to share what God had done in his life, and God began to use his preaching in a mighty way. Over the next several years, God sent him on three missionary journeys to spread the gospel and plant new churches. Talk about a transformation! This man had gone from church persecutor to church planter. So when he writes to the church in Rome, he says, "I am not ashamed of the gospel; it is the power of God for salvation to everyone who has faith..."

Perhaps you are not ashamed of the gospel, either, but are you proud of it? Is the good news about Jesus Christ the most important fact to you? If not, why isn't it? What keeps you from being consumed by the fact that Jesus Christ came to this earth to bring hope and peace and salvation to all? What keeps you from giving away the good news at every opportunity?

I think three things may prevent us from talking about Jesus. Perhaps the first one is peer pressure. We don't want people to think badly about us and we don't want to be embarrassed, so we just keep the good news to ourselves. Perhaps the second reason is that we believe other things are more important to share. The third reason may be a concern for personal rights. We may not want to infringe on anyone else's beliefs, so we just keep our beliefs a secret.

Of course, Satan has none of these problems. Satan doesn't care about peer pressure. He doesn't care about anyone's rights. And he wants to tell his story to everybody. So the servants of Satan talk (wittingly or unwittingly) about his schemes, his triumphs, and his priorities everywhere they go.

What about us? Are we consumed by the good news of the Savior? Does it encapsulate our lives? Is it our total being? Do we find ourselves talking with perfect strangers about Jesus Christ?

We naturally talk about things we consider to be important. I saw this quite clearly a few months ago when I bought a new truck. I had already bought a used fifth wheel for camping and needed a truck to tow it. I was preaching down in Alabama, and on Sunday morning I was exchanging small talk with the sound man. I said, "What kind of work do you do?"

He said, "I teach high school—and I sell used cars."

"Really?" I said. "I'm looking for a truck."

"Well, maybe I can help you out. I sold 849 cars last year."

"And you're part time?" I asked.

"Yes," he said. "I teach school."

Anyway, about two weeks after I came home, I called him and said, "Have you found me a truck?" About every two weeks, I asked the same thing: "Have you found me a truck?"

Finally, Martha and I were on our way down to Florida, so I called him again and said, "Hey, have you found me a truck?"

"No," he said, "but I want you to stop at the Ford dealership here. He'll make you a real good deal." Sure enough, the Ford dealer offered me a very good deal on a truck, and that's what I'm driving today.

When I went back to Indiana, everybody wanted to know about my truck. It became a conversation piece. "Tell us about your truck," they'd say. "How'd you get that truck?" This went on for six or seven weeks, every place I went: "Tell us about your truck." Nobody said, "Tell us about Jesus."

I began to think about that. When we engage people in conversation, we normally talk about something that's important to us. We talk about our grandkids because they are important to us. We talk about our work or we talk about our favorite sports team. But where in the priority of our topics of conversation is Jesus? Is he even on our list?

Do you or I ever go all day without talking about Jesus? If so, we are not consumed with the good news like the apostle Paul was, because every place he went, he told people about Jesus. It didn't matter who they were, friend or foe. He told them about Jesus.

When the good news of Jesus Christ consumes Christians, the church is alive and dynamic. I've done a lot of traveling around the country for the past ten years, and I've made notes about the people and congregations I've visited. Now I can pretty much walk into a church and tell you whether the people are spiritually alive or dead. (Or on life support!) You probably can do that, too. When I walk into churches that are full of spiritual vitality, I want to know why. And I have noticed that those dynamic congregations share four common traits.

Trait 1: Talking about Jesus

The first trait of a dynamic church is that they talk about Jesus—a lot! In their worship services, you will hear these people say, "Let me tell you what Jesus is doing in my life." In other words, they give you their testimony. When was the last time you did that? (We used to do that in Wednesday night worship services. Now we don't have Wednesday night services, so I don't know when you do it.) What has the Lord been doing for you? How is your life different because of Jesus Christ? In churches that are growing and dynamic, everybody—from pastor to laypeople—freely talks about Jesus. They are consumed by the gospel. "Let me tell you what happened in church yesterday," they say. "This family got saved or this person got healed." They get excited telling the story of what Jesus is doing.

Do you have a story to tell about Jesus? Do you have a story that would give God honor and glory and praise? We can sing wonderful songs about the love of Christ, but the people we meet want to know what difference he has made in our own lives.

I have found that if you share something good with another person, they are likely to share it with at least seven other people. But if you share something bad, they'll share it with at least thirteen other people! Now start doing the math. Let's say you run into ten people today and you tell each of them what the Lord is doing in your life. Let's say you are consumed by the gospel, so you give your testimony to ten people and each of them share it with seven others. That's seventy people who have been influenced in a single day by your testimony. Well, let's assume you tell those ten people some gossip about someone. Then each of them shares it with thirteen other people. Wow! That's the power of a testimony.

Throughout the New Testament, when Jesus encountered the people, he sought to enter into their lives and respond to their needs.

After each encounter, the people left rejoicing and testifying. In Mark 5, we have the story of the demon-possessed man. After Jesus delivered him of the demon, "he went away and began to proclaim...how much Jesus had done for him" (v 20). In this case, the individual man went away rejoicing. A little later in Mark 7, Jesus healed the deaf and mute man. Verse 36 says, "Jesus ordered them to tell no one; but the more he ordered them, the more zealously they proclaimed it." Now we see the crowds were so amazed by what he did that they began to tell the story.

We sometimes think nothing spectacular has happened to us, so we do not have a story to tell. Yet our society is filled with people telling other people's stories. Does it have to happen to you for you to rejoice and be glad? I think not. Let's look for the stories of God's redemptive actions in our world and proclaim them.

First John 1:1 says, "We declare to you what was from the beginning, what we have heard, what we have seen with our eyes, what we have looked at and touched with our hands, concerning the word of life." When people see you, do they hear a glowing advertisement for Jesus? That's characteristic of a dynamic Christian and of a dynamic church.

Trait 2: Caring for One Another

The second thing I find in dynamic churches is that they care deeply about one another. They go beyond just being kind and hospitable; they do things to help one another. They share one another's burdens. They come to one another's rescue. They are there to encourage and wrap arms of comfort around others, to speak words of faith and hope into their lives, to help them when they're struggling with life's most difficult moments. They don't ask permission; they just come and love on them.

Have you ever longed for somebody to hug you and encourage you? Did you ever want someone to put his or her arms around you and say, "I'm so proud of you. I'm so glad you are walking in the way of Jesus Christ. I'm so glad that you have been called by God to this ministry and you have responded to that call"? Dynamic churches are places where people care deeply about each other and express it openly. Why? Because they have the love of Christ Jesus within them.

The early church as recorded in Acts, especially the first few chapters, was a group of believers who had experienced Pentecost and who believed that Jesus was going to return in their lifetime. They believed he was going to return because Jesus said to them, "Truly I tell you, there are some standing here who will not taste death until they see that the kingdom of God has come with power"(Mark 9:1). Consequently, they had changed their normal routine (Acts 2:42–47). Today, we recognize this period as very special in the development of the early church, yet it offers to us a principle of care and concern that continues in the fabric of dynamic church bodies today.

Trait 3: Serving the Community

Third, dynamic churches serve their communities with compassion. They don't say, "We've got this nice little group and we are so happy that we don't want anyone else to come in." They don't think, "We are so happy. We're so blessed. And we're keeping it all to ourselves." That's not what the Word of God says to do. The Word says God blesses us to bless others, so a dynamic church looks for ways to bless the surrounding community.

We should speak into the hearts, minds, and lives of those who are in need. We should not run away from drug addicts; we should run to them because we have the gospel, and we know the gospel changes people's lives! We should not run away from unwed mothers, child molesters, or pornography peddlers. Those are the people Christ died for, people who are hurting and lost.

You see, the word *lost* means more than being spiritually lost. It means a person is lost in this life. A lost person could say, "I don't know what I'm doing. I'm all messed up." Being the church means dealing with messy people at times. It means we have to handle other people's stuff.

Look at the New Testament account of Jesus' ministry. What did the Pharisees and Sadducees accuse him of? "You eat with publicans and sinners." Absolutely he did, because he came "to seek out and to save the lost" (Luke 19:10). That's our calling as well.

Back in 1980, I was serving on the pastoral staff of Park Place Church of God in Anderson, Indiana. One of our men said, "I'd like you to conduct a worship service at the National Guard Armory."

I said, "Okay, let's find a date and I'd be glad to go."

So I went the next Sunday morning at seven o'clock and held a thirty-minute worship service for them. The next month, they called and said, "Can you come back?" And I said, "Sure."

At Park Place, I was ministering to a group of people who were involved in national church work, teaching at the college, and serving in other significant places of leadership. The persons in the national guard displayed a wider variety of vocations, and many of them had no church connection at all. But they needed Jesus Christ, so I went. That began a twenty-five-year period of military chaplaincy for me—putting myself into the lives of lost people so that I could share a word of hope with them.

We like to sing the hymn "Just As I Am," but sometimes we act as though we do not believe what it says:

Just as I am, without one plea,
But that Thy blood was shed for me,
And that Thou bid'st me come to Thee—
O Lamb of God, I come, I come![3]

Instead we say, "Get yourself cleaned up and come to church. Don't bring your stuff in with you; leave it outside." That's not what the hymn says, and it's not what the Word says. When we begin to serve our communities with compassion, our churches will become dynamic places of healing.

Trait 4: Business Done Biblically

The fourth thing I have noticed about dynamic churches is that they deal with their business in a biblical manner. Now we all know that a congregation has to do a certain amount of business, but we use so many dysfunctional methods to do business in the church that it

---

3. Charlotte Elliott, "Just As I Am," *Worship the Lord: Hymnal of the Church of God* (Anderson, IN: Warner Press, 1989), no. 402.

creates havoc. It's time we stop this idiocy. It is time that we begin to conduct our church business in a biblical manner.

The church was not created to become a laughingstock for the rest of the community. But as I travel around the country, I hear of one church fight after another arising from doing business in an unbiblical, unhealthy, and devilish manner. We need to call a stop to this.

One of Charles Shultz's comic strips shows a character holding a Bible and a pair of scissors, cutting out pages. Someone asks, "What are you doing?" The character says, "I'm getting a Bible I can live by." We don't have that option. We cannot pick and choose what parts of God's Word we will obey. We have been given a message and a mandate to share that message with the rest of the world. If we bring disrepute on the gospel by the way we conduct ourselves in the local church, we will have to give an account before the throne of God.

Are you consumed by the gospel, or are you ashamed of it? I don't think many of us are ashamed of it. But I'm not convinced that we are consumed by it either. Not like the apostle Paul was consumed. He said:

> Five times I have received from the Jews the forty lashes minus one. Three times I was beaten with rods. Once I received a stoning. Three times I was shipwrecked; for a night and a day I was adrift at sea; on frequent journeys, in danger from rivers, danger from bandits, danger from my own people, danger from Gentiles, danger in the city, danger in the wilderness, danger at sea, danger from false brothers and sisters; in toil and hardship, through many a sleepless night, hungry and thirsty, often without food, cold and naked. And, besides other things, I am under daily pressure because of my anxiety for all the churches...
>
> I am content with weaknesses, insults, hardships, persecutions, and calamities for the sake of Christ; for whenever I am weak, then I am strong. (2 Cor 11:24–28; 12:10)

I have three challenges for you. First, will you tell someone in the next twenty-four hours what Jesus Christ means to you? Second, will you review the characteristics of a dynamic church, and if they are not true of your church, will you ask the Lord, "What do you want me to do to help change this?" Finally, will you pray honestly, "Lord, am I the problem?" I guarantee that the Holy Spirit will answer that prayer. And if you find that you are holding your congregation back from all that Christ has created his church to be, then fall on your knees and ask for forgiveness. Ask for wisdom and guidance. I am sure the Lord will answer that prayer too.

Throughout my ministerial career, I have had the glorious honor of serving with some fantastic saints who have taught me many spiritual lessons. All churches go through periods when some issue becomes the focal point of discussion and personal opinions are expressed with gusto at times. One such occasion occurred when we as a congregation had made the decision under the leadership of the Holy Spirit to relocate to property the church had purchased years before.

Many ideas were shared about what was to be built, the design, the cost, the quality, and many other issues. One saint stood at one of the congregational meetings and expressed a strong opinion about the resources being allocated to the Christian education ministry. At the conclusion of the comments, she then said, "Now that is what I think and believe, but I am open to the leading of the Holy Spirit to change my mind, and I certainly do not want to be a stumbling block to this congregation. Furthermore, my financial commitment to the project stays regardless of the outcome." As her pastor, I was elated by her spiritual depth and profound love for her church and fellow Christians, such love that she was not willing to hold them hostage over what she thought should be done. This kind of personal honesty and commitment to the whole strengthens the body of Christ.

Don't be ashamed of the gospel. As Christians, we have a great heritage. Let's live up to it.

Chapter 4

Unwavering Faith

For this reason it depends on faith, in order that the promise may rest on grace and be guaranteed to all his descendants, not only to the adherents of the law but also to those who share the faith of Abraham (for he is the father of all of us)...Hoping against hope, he believed that he would become "the father of many nations," according to what was said, "So numerous shall your descendants be." He did not weaken in faith when he considered his own body, which was already as good as dead (for he was about a hundred years old), or when he considered the barrenness of Sarah's womb.

—Romans 4:16, 18–19

Unwavering faith is the cornerstone for the fulfillment of God's will. Think about that. The apostle Paul says that Abraham "did not waver through unbelief regarding the promise of God, but was strengthened in his faith and gave glory to God" (Rom 4:20 NIV).

Now we must go to the book of Genesis to understand what this text is really saying. Genesis 12–21 covers a period of about twenty-five years when the patriarch was known as Abram. He was seventy-five years old when God said to him, "I want you to leave your land and go to another place." God told him to leave Haran and go to another country. He promised Abram at that moment that a great nation would arise from his offspring.

In chapter 15, after Abram had left his home country and traveled afar, he reminded God, "Hey, I don't have a son. Who's going to inherit everything? How are you going to make this happen in my life?" He was still faithful, but he questioned how God could fulfill his promise.

In Genesis 17, God confirms his covenant with Abram and changes his name to Abraham. He also changes his wife Sarai's name to Sarah. Finally, in chapter 21, their son Isaac is born. From the time

God gave Abram this wonderful promise to its fulfillment, twenty-five years elapsed.

We easily lose sight of how Abram's faith was tested during that time. We may say, "Well, he surely could have believed God for twenty-five years. There would be no problem with that." But consider what else happened to Abram during those years.

Genesis 12 says that he went to Egypt to escape a great famine. His wife Sarai was really a knock-out, so he said to her, "Lie. Tell them you're my sister or they'll take you away from me." Genesis 13 tells how Abram and his nephew Lot had a family feud because their herdsmen were fighting over land and water rights. Then Lot gets into trouble and Abram rescues him. In Genesis 15, Abram asks God to confirm his covenant—but he does not do that right away. So Genesis 16 describes how Abram had a son by his wife's servant Hagar. We know the mess that came out of that. In Genesis 17, God did renew his covenant with the sign of circumcision and a name change. So they lived happily ever after, right?

Not quite. In Genesis 18, Abraham pleads that God not destroy the wicked city of Sodom because that's where his nephew lives. In chapter 19, Sodom and Gomorrah are destroyed, but Lot's family is delivered. Then Lot has an incestuous relationship with his daughters. And in Genesis 20, Abraham crosses swords with King Abimelech. After all those trials and false starts, Isaac is born in chapter 21. The promises of God do not keep us from having to deal with life's problems.

We American Christians have assumed that if our faith is the right kind of faith, we won't have problems. But that's not in God's Word, is it? We tell ourselves that if we're not healed, not delivered from destructive habits, or whatever, it must be because we lack faith. But that's not what God's Word says. It is true that we must have unwavering faith in God's promises, as Abraham had, but God is not tied to our timetable, and **God's promises do not exempt us from trouble.**

As I travel around the country, I encounter many people who tell me about the stuff in their lives. They want to have hope and they want to be encouraged, but there is so much troubling stuff in their lives. That stuff causes them to question their faith. It can even grind down their determination to follow the Lord. Why is that?

Doubting God's Promises

Why do we doubt God's promises? I believe there are several reasons.

First, we may doubt God's promises because they seem to take too long to be fulfilled. Abraham and Sarah waited twenty-five years for the child of promise to be born. God delayed the blessed event until Abraham and Sarah were pushing the century mark. So when the promise was fulfilled, they knew it was not just a good thing; it was a God thing.

Abraham doubted God while he waited. That's why he conceived a son by Hagar. But he kept on journeying toward the Promised Land as God had commanded, and he was eventually rewarded for that.

Second, we may doubt God's promises because we do not really know them. We are biblically illiterate. This is a growing problem in America, as I saw recently on an airplane flight from the West Coast to the East Coast. It was a midnight flight, so most of the passengers just wanted to sleep; but I sat down by a young man and began working on a sermon, referring to my Bible.

"What are you doing?" he asked.

It should have been obvious, but I said, "I'm reading the Bible."

"I've never read the Bible," he said.

"Excuse me?"

"I've never read the Bible," he said again.

"You don't know John 3:16?" I asked.

"No."

I said, "Don't you watch football? A guy stands at every end zone and holds up a placard with John 3:16." I thought this young fellow was putting me on, but after talking with him for fifteen minutes or so, I realized he wasn't. He had never read the Bible and knew nothing about what it contained.

A lot of Americans have never read the Bible, and many of us who have read it don't really know what it says. Do you know the Bible's promises for you? Could you name one hundred promises that are in the Bible for you? There are far more than that, but can you name at least one hundred of them? God has given us many promises in the written Word to bolster our faith.

Abraham didn't have the Scriptures, but we do. If we claim the promises in God's Word, if we appropriate them for ourselves, then we will see them fulfilled. But many good church folks do not even know these promises, so they doubt the love of God.

Third, we may doubt God's promises because Satan uses our emotions to discredit God. "Well, you have this promise," the Adversary says. "God said he would be with you and take care of you, but where is he? God said he would do this—why hasn't he?"

Do you suppose the Adversary said anything to Abraham during those twenty-five years that he had to deal with the stuff of life? Of course, he did. Yet Scripture says that "he did not waver through unbelief concerning the promises of God." How was this possible? How is it possible for us? How can we have unwavering faith in spite of our doubts and questions?

Steps to Unwavering Faith

I believe the first step is to firmly establish your identity in God through Jesus Christ. When "your life is hidden with Christ in God" (Col 3:3), the stuff of this world really is not about you. Your victory over the stuff is not your achievement either; it's what Christ does in you. You can establish your identity with Christ by accepting his invitation: "Come to me, all you that are weary and are carrying heavy burdens, and I will give you rest" (Matt 11:28). The psalmist says, "As far as the east is from the west, so far he removes our transgressions from us" (Ps 103:12). It is hard for some people to accept this idea. It is difficult for them to imagine that their old life can be swallowed up in the sinless, eternal life of Christ. But if you will find your identity in him, your faith can stand firm in life's storms.

The second step is to claim God's promises as your own. Herbert Lockyer wrote a classic book titled *All the Promises of the Bible*. He found several thousand promises in the Bible. (So you see, it really was not far-fetched for me to expect you to know one hundred!) Tell me, which of God's promises support and undergird you every day?

When a man and woman stand in front of a minister and pledge their love to each other in marriage, they make some important promises. They promise to take care of each other when they grow old. They promise to stand by one another in health and sickness. Perhaps you have exchanged such vows with someone. If so, as you claimed those promises, you began to trust that person. To be sure, sometimes the marriage vows are broken. When they are, lives are damaged. Trusting people are hurt. Sorrowful consequences follow them for years because their promises were broken.

Yet God never breaks a promise. Never, never, never! Proverbs 3:5–6 says, "Trust in the Lord with all your heart, and do not rely on your own insight. In all your ways acknowledge him, and he will make straight your paths."

Fifty years ago, a minister was preaching on that text on a hot summer night at Camp Lurecrest, North Carolina. He said, "Would you claim this promise of God for your life, and what he might call you to do?" A young boy came from eight rows back to kneel at an altar of prayer and say, "I believe that promise." I was that boy. And I said, "Lord, whatever you want me to do, I'll do." I had been saved at age nine, but that night I appropriated God's promise to direct my path. I have lived the rest of my life according to that promise.

Certainly, a lot of discouraging things have happened to me, but God's promise has never failed. Ever since I claimed his promise, I have prayed time and again, "This must be in your will, O Lord, or I will not do it." That has become a life promise for me and my wife Martha. When we got married, we said, "We claim this promise together. Wherever the Lord leads us, that's where we're going."

Perhaps you don't know one hundred of God's promises for you. What about five? Ask yourself, What five promises of God am I willing to base my life on? What five promises of God's Word will direct my path? What five promises will I cling to, when the pressures of this world threaten to destroy me?

Perhaps you can't think of five promises, so what about one? Abraham had one promise: "I will make of you a great nation." He based the rest of his life on that single promise, and look at the outcome.

Think about the thing that is troubling you most right now. Identify it clearly in your mind. Now find a promise of God for that struggle in his Holy Word. Find one promise that answers the problem that threatens to defeat your faith and repeat that promise every time the problem confronts you. Just repeat that one promise of God and see what a difference it makes.

Tell somebody about your struggle, and then tell them God's promise you have claimed for your struggle. It's all right to admit you are being tested, because we all will have struggles in this life, but we also have God's Word to see us through them. I am convinced that God's people seldom claim what already belongs to them, yet God's Word is full of "his precious and very great promises" to sustain us every day (2 Peter 1:4).

I believe the third step to an unwavering faith is to view life through the lens of God's promises. When I became general director at Church of God Ministries, some of my friends said, "You are the dumbest guy we know. Why would anyone want to take this job?"

I said, "I'm not taking a job, I'm following the leading of the Lord." I wasn't looking for a job, because I already had one. But the Lord called me to do this for him, so I knew I could claim his promise to answer that call. The challenges and problems of the assignment appeared completely different when seen through the lens of his promises.

One of my favorite promises is recorded in the book of Joshua. Moses was about to die and Joshua was being called to take his place as leader of the nation. God said to Joshua, "I will be with you. I will not leave you nor forsake you. Be strong and of good courage" (Josh 1:5b–6a NKJV). God didn't say it just once or twice; he said it three times. Was Joshua hard of hearing? I don't think so. I believe God repeated it to emphasize the trustworthiness of the promise he had made.

Why do we have so much emotional dysfunction in the life of the church today? Why do church people become upset over the most trivial things? I believe it's because we are not seeing life through the promises of God.

We can be strong and courageous, no matter what challenges we face. We have no need to be terrified. We need not be discouraged, for the Lord God is with us wherever we go. *Wherever we go.* We cannot go anywhere that God has not already been—and has already prepared the way for us.

Here's another marvelous promise. Jesus said, "I came that they may have life, and have it abundantly" (John 10:10b). An abundant life means one that has God's generous supply for every need. An abundant life doesn't mean that you won't have to deal with troublesome stuff, but it does mean you will have God's provision as you deal with it. And that's an important difference.

I challenge you to reread your Bible and underline some promises that will become your window on the world. On what promises will you base your life? In light of what promises will you make your life decisions? I believe the Lord will bless you if you claim his Word as your own, and live your life in light of it. On the rock of his Word you can build an unwavering faith.

Chapter 5

Grace for Difficult Questions

Since we have been justified through faith, we have peace with God through our Lord Jesus Christ, through whom we have gained access by faith into this grace in which we now stand. And we rejoice in the hope of the glory of God. Not only so, but we also rejoice in our sufferings, because we know that suffering produces perseverance; perseverance, character; and character, hope. And hope does not disappoint us, because God has poured out his love into our hearts by the Holy Spirit, whom he has given us.

—Romans 5:1–5 NIV

The Roman church was a very young church, in need of guidance, wisdom, and support. The apostle Paul wanted to go there and provide that support, but circumstances prevented that for several years. In the meantime, he wrote a letter under the influence of the Holy Spirit so that the Roman Christians would have something to help them develop their spiritual maturity. Remember, they did not have the New Testament. They had heard the testimony of other believers, so they were anxious to gain all Christian instruction that might come their way. They had many, many questions—probably more than you and I have—and they were eager to get answers.

So Paul tells them to rejoice in their sufferings. I am sure they did not expect to hear that, but Paul knew this small, fledgling group of believers needed to hear it. And he packs much more into these five verses. Let's unpack some of it and see what Paul would say to us.

In chapter 4, he recounted how Abraham's faith had justified him before God. Now Paul says to the church at Rome, and he says to us, "You are justified by your faith in God's grace." Because we are justified, we now have peace with God.

Now when the New Testament and the Old Testament speak of peace, the word means more than the absence of conflict. In the Old Testament, the Hebrew word for peace was *shalom*. This particular word means "the fullness of God, the harmonious relationship with God." When we have this kind of peace, we are not at odds with God; we stand in his presence and receive his fullness in our lives. So when someone says, "Shalom!," to you, they desire for you to experience God's fullness and to be comfortable in his presence.

Have you ever visited a home where you did not feel you were welcome? Ever visited a family where you felt there was no peace? Have you gone into someone's home and found it to be comfy and relaxed, as if it were your own? In such a home, you said, "Ahhh, this feels good. I like this." Paul says to the Christians in Rome that because they have been justified by faith in God and because the grace of God now rests upon them, they are at home with God. They have peace in their hearts, no matter what is happening in their external world.

You see, Paul wants us to be concerned with our inner life because we can't control much of our external circumstances. We may think we have control, but then something unexpected happens and our world is turned upside down. We realize we are not in control after all. We can only control our internal response to what happens. So as Paul prepared the Roman Christians to deal with difficult problems in their lives, he turned their attention inward. If their hearts were troubled, they would have trouble dealing with their external circumstances. A person's internal life must be at peace.

Justified before God

How do we get there? We get there by having faith in God, who justifies us and sends his grace into our hearts. His grace confirms that we have right standing with him, and that knowledge will hold us steady in the face of adversity. So, the first result of being justified is that we know we are at peace with God.

Some people are afraid of God. When I was nine years old, I had gone to church a lot. I went to church when my parents didn't go. I sat on the front row and sang every hymn because I loved to sing. One night, the pastor preached on hell fire and damnation. He scared me to death. Then I went home, watched the *Ed Sullivan Show*, and went to bed. By midnight, I still hadn't fallen asleep. I was afraid I was going to burn in hell. So I got up, went to my parents' room, and said, "I need to be saved right now because I don't want to burn." I was afraid of God.

They knelt with me there, I prayed the sinner's prayer, and the Lord came into my life. Then I said, "I want to call the pastor."

"It's one o'clock," my parents told me.

"I don't care. He kept me up, so I'm getting him up."

We called the pastor and of course he rejoiced. The Scriptures say that the angels in heaven were rejoicing that night, so I wanted him to rejoice too. But I have to admit, I got converted because I was afraid of God.

By age fifteen, I had learned to love God, not just be afraid of him. I began to have a relationship with God that superseded my fears. Then I began to have peace with God.

That's what Paul wanted the Christians at Rome to have, not merely a fear of God (although all of us should fear, honor, and respect God), but a relationship of love and trust. You and I can have such a relationship with the Lord because his grace has come into our lives. We know we are now justified before him. We know he wanted to save us because he loves us so much.

Access to God's Grace

Paul says we have access to God's grace, not just the first time we call upon him, but every time. We have continual access to him. Let me read it again: "Since we have been justified through faith, we have peace with God through our Lord Jesus Christ, through whom we have gained access by faith into this grace in which we now stand." This is an amazing thought.

Suppose I asked, "Do you have access to the president of the United States?" You probably would say, "No, I don't think I do."

Suppose I asked, "Do you have access to your pastor?" "Well, certainly on Sundays," you might say.

But our access to God is continual. He is always available to those who love him. And that means his grace is always available to comfort, sustain, heal, and forgive us.

When I became general director at Church of God Ministries, I called five people who had been an inspiration to me. I said, "I want to give you three A's. I want to give you *access* to me anytime you want it. I want to give you the right to *advise* me. And, if necessary, you have the right to *admonish* me." These were my spiritual elders, and they all agreed. Three of them have passed away now, but their role in my ministry has been invaluable. They had a formative influence upon me because they always had access to me and I had access to them.

Our text says, "Since we have been justified through faith...we have gained access by faith into this grace in which we now stand." All of us need God's grace, and we can give each other his grace.

Confidence in God's Power

What did the young church at Rome need? They didn't need a building or a professional staff. But they lived in the midst of life's "stuff," so they needed access to an all-powerful Father to help them deal with it all. Because they were justified, they had access to God, and that access encouraged their hearts.

Paul says, "We rejoice in the hope of the glory of God." *Rejoice* is another word for "having confidence." So we have confidence in God, knowing that he is all-powerful to act on our behalf. If we're going to deal with life's difficult problems, we need this inner confidence in his power. We need to know that God is not against us; he is for us.

So far, Paul's progression seems pretty simple: First, we are justified. Second, we have access to God's grace. Third, we have confidence in God's power. But then he makes an abrupt turn and says, "Not only so, but we also rejoice in our sufferings."

Wait a minute, Paul. We weren't talking about suffering. We were talking about God's grace and peace and power, so why did you jump into suffering? How do you expect us to deal with that?

Actually, the foundation of our ability to deal with suffering is this peace with God, this confidence in God's power that grows out of our relationship with God. If that peace and confidence is not within us, we cannot deal with our suffering. Paul reminds us that we are justified by faith; the grace of God has entered our lives, so we now experience the peace of God and have confidence in God's ability to care for us. If that's our position, we can deal with suffering.

When Martha and I were first married, we lived in a college apartment, and one night we thought somebody was breaking in downstairs. I grabbed my baseball bat and began to sneak down the stairs. (Martha was right behind me. She whispered, "Don't leave me here!") I don't know what I would have done with that bat if I found somebody, but it felt good to hold in my hand.

We went down the stairs, stopped, and listened. All we could hear was our hearts pounding. We finally flipped on the light switch and nobody was there, so we relaxed. We had been somewhat afraid but not frightened. I remembered that night as I began to face some of the scarier issues of life. I realized that it is normal to be somewhat afraid when I grapple with those issues—even with physical suffering—but I do not need to be frightened, because I have the peace of God in my life.

Suffering Leads to...

But that's not the end. Notice the next step of faith that Paul describes. He says that if we have the peace of God within us, our sufferings will develop perseverance.

Perseverance means we are able to stand because we know that we live in the presence of God. We have all of God's resources on our side. We are not dealing with our trials, our temptations, or our sufferings on the basis of our own ingenuity or strength. We persevere because the peace of God flows through us. The grace of God sustains us. The power of God surrounds us. So we know we can face anything. We begin to look at our most painful "stuff" from God's perspective.

If we were to express Paul's argument with a mathematical formula, it might look something like this:

$$SSTQ \div G = PCH$$

"SSTQ" stands for the suffering, stuff, trials, and questions of life. Romans 5 says that when they are divided by the peace of God (G), they yield perseverance, character, and hope (PCH).

Now all of us live with SSTQ, don't we? I don't know why some of us have stuff all the time and others have stuff just now and then. Maybe it's a result of the decisions we make. Some of us make good decisions all the time, while others make good decisions half the time. If we make good decisions only half the time, we have many more painful consequences to live with. (After all, there's nothing wrong with making a bad decision, but we've got to live with the consequences.) Regardless of the reasons, all of us have a certain amount of stuff—suffering, trials, and questions. The peace of God enables us to deal with it. The peace of God brings insight into problems that seem to have no solution. When it does, we can rejoice (i.e., we can have confidence), even in the midst of our sufferings. The epistle of James says the same thing:

> My brothers and sisters, whenever you face trials of any kind, consider it nothing but joy, because you know that the testing of your faith produces endurance; and let endurance have its full effect, so that you may be mature and complete, lacking in nothing. (James 1:2–4)

When we deal with life's stuff in God's way, not our way, we become more spiritually mature and complete. The indwelling peace of God enables us to face the most daunting troubles and say, How will God be glorified through this?

Years ago, I had a friend named Larry, a middle-aged man who contracted leukemia. Doctors told him he had one year to live. One year to live! His friends wondered how he would deal with it.

Larry was a layman in our church. He began to testify about the way God was using the prospect of death to help him grow spiritually. Pretty soon, he was invited to all sorts of places to tell his story. By the time he died, he had shared it with over ten thousand people—prisoners, people on skid row, college students, and church members. All because he was able to see his predicament through the eyes of God.

I'm sure Larry didn't want to die young. He didn't want to leave his family. But he looked at that year of suffering as an opportunity to grow in Christ and encourage others to have faith. "The only difference between me and you," he would say, "is that the doctors think they know when I'm going to die. You will too, but you don't know when." He would joke about it.

I conducted Larry's funeral. It was a time of such rejoicing for his family that I cannot adequately describe it. Why were they rejoicing? Because they had encountered death in the presence of God. They were dealing with tragedy in the presence of God.

In recent years, I've done this when I had to deal with an overwhelming problem. I've said, "Okay, God, you sit in my chair and I'll go over there and sit on the other side of the desk." I physically do that. And then I say, "Now, God, how should we approach this?"

The Bible says I have immediate access to the Father. I have his grace and peace surrounding me, no matter what is happening to me. The Bible promises me that, and you have the same promise.

Stilling Our Anxious Hearts

One of the great challenges for every person of faith is to match what they believe in their mind and soul with the reality of the circumstances of the day. From the beginning of the Old Testament through the end of the New Testament, individuals who made it into sacred writ have had to deal with this issue. Today, we know that we have various personality types within the human family. These personality types all respond differently to the same set of life's stimuli. But Scripture tells us, "Do not worry about anything, but in everything by prayer and supplication with thanksgiving let your requests be made known to God. And the peace of God, which surpasses all understanding, will guard your hearts and your minds in Christ Jesus" (Phil 4:6–7). This requires different responses from the various personality types.

We know, in broad terms, that left-brain responses are normally categorized as logic and right brain responses as feelings. The difficulty for many personality types is the cognitive dissonance between these two—right and left—when addressing faith issues.

I may want to believe or really believe, but my present circumstances are overwhelming. I pray and trust God for the result, but seemingly nothing changes. How can I still believe if I do not see changes. This is the first hurdle of practicing our faith and hope in the promises of God. In other words, I must come to the inner conclusion in mind and heart that I will trust God and his promises if the worst of the worst happens to me (see the book of Job). The reason Abraham was willing to follow God's directive to sacrifice Isaac (Gen 22) was that he had come to this crucial life decision: I will trust God above all else!

The second hurdle is perseverance, or staying the course. Our American society is characterized by instant gratification. This runs counter to faith and hope. If I immediately get what I desire, then there is no requirement for faith in my hope. In most hymnals today, you find the hymn "Standing on the Promises," written in 1886 by Russell K. Carter. Stanza two states,

> Standing on the promises that cannot fail,
> When the howling storms of doubt and fear assail,
> By the living Word of God I shall prevail,
> Standing on the promises of God.

Regardless of personality type, where you were born, or your present circumstances, at some point you will have to make a decision and stick with it. For the believer in Jesus Christ, it is the renewing each day, or moment if necessary, of that decision to follow Christ and take up the cross.

I have found that the more I am dealing with difficult circumstances and feel weak in my faith, the more I need to remind myself of my relationship and dependence on Christ (2 Cor 12:10). When I visit the gym four or five times a week doing a rather strenuous physical routine, my stamina and strength increase; yet right after a strenuous workout, I am somewhat weak because of the physical exertion. I recover within a few hours, but I then want to rest. This is also true in the spiritual arena of life. When you are dealing with life's issues and faith in Christ is challenged, you will become temporarily exhausted or weakened, but hang on: you actually are getting stronger.

The Word's Life-Changing Power

Allow the power of God's Word to sustain you. Second Timothy 3:16–17 says, "All scripture is inspired[4] by God and is useful for teaching, for reproof, for correction, and for training in righteousness, so that everyone who belongs to God may be proficient, equipped for every good work." Second Timothy 2:15 says, "Do your best to present yourself to God as one approved by him, a worker who has no need to be ashamed, rightly explaining the word of truth." Hebrews 4:12 says, "Indeed, the word of God is living and active, sharper than any two-edged sword, piercing until it divides soul from spirit, joints from marrow; it is able to judge the thoughts and intentions of the heart." You can deal with life's most difficult stuff when you have the peace of God. And you have God's peace because you have access to his grace. His Word says so.

Claim the Word as your own. Stand on it and enjoy the privileges that it promises. Know with absolute confidence that God will take care of you.

You may be saying, "That's all right for you, but my faith is pretty weak. I am pushed around by life's troubles. I have no stability. I'm up, I'm down, I'm like a roller coaster. Something comes along

---

4. The Greek word translated "inspired" is *theopneustos*. It literally means that Scripture is "God-breathed."

and just knocks me off my faith." If that's how you feel, review this chapter and see if you have "the peace of God, which surpasses all understanding" (Phil 4:7) flowing in your heart and soul.

Jesus usually answered his critics in one of two ways. He either asked them a question or he quoted them a scripture. He faced the same kind of things you and I face—questions, struggles, trials, and all kinds of stuff. But he had the Word of God deeply implanted in his heart and mind to help him through those difficult times.

The psalmist said, "I treasure your word in my heart, so that I may not sin against you" (Ps 119:11). How is your supply of the Word? Do you have enough spiritual fuel in your tank? An indicator light on my new truck tells me when I'm running low on fuel. It says, You have so many miles to go and this puppy will stop! Well, we stop spiritually when we fail to put the Word into our lives consistently. If you wonder why you are having difficulty dealing with life's stuff, it may be because your spiritual tank is running low. If so, I challenge you to fill your mind and heart with the Word of God.

Chapter 6

Placed in the Body of Christ

For by the grace given to me I say to everyone among you not to think of yourself more highly than you ought to think, but to think with sober judgment, each according to the measure of faith that God has assigned. For as in one body we have many members, and not all the members have the same function, so we, who are many, are one body in Christ, and individually we are members one of another. We have gifts that differ according to the grace given to us: prophecy, in proportion to faith; ministry, in ministering; the teacher, in teaching; the exhorter, in exhortation; the giver, in generosity; the leader, in diligence; the compassionate, in cheerfulness. —Romans 12:3–8

Your faith in Christ places you in the church, the body of Christ, where you have certain rights, privileges, and responsibilities. Paul is writing in this context to the church at Rome. Remember that this is a new church, so they do not know much about life in the church. They do not have the benefit of two thousand years of church history. So Paul is trying to describe for them the divine design of the church. We need to understand this same design if we are to understand our God-ordained role in the church.

"We, who are many, are one body in Christ." This church belongs to Christ, and inside of his church are many distinctive groups. They include the Church of the Nazarene, the Church of God, the Wesleyan Church, and every faith group that seeks to serve and represent the Lord Jesus Christ in this world. The church includes your local congregation and every born-again believer who's in it. Remember, this is not my church or your church; this is God's church, and God places those of us who are saved into his church to do what he wants us to do.

All believers are united in Christ, so Christ is the head of the church. Colossians 1:18 ("And he [Christ] is the head of the body, the church") and many other scriptures declare it. In order for us to understand our role in the church, we must first understand that we belong to Christ. Christ is our Lord and the focus of our worldview. Christ is our head.

Each disciple is different, yet our differences should support and strengthen the total body of the church, not create division. Paul develops this theme in 1 Corinthians 12, where he says, "To each is given the manifestation of the Spirit for the common good" (v 7). Peter expresses this same theme in 1 Peter 4:10, "Like good stewards of the manifold grace of God, serve one another with whatever gift each of you has received." The next time you attend a Christian worship service, look around. No two people there will be exactly the same size, of the same appearance, or in the same frame of mind. Yet all of those differences can be beneficial to the entire church body.

My wife and grandchildren love jigsaw puzzles, so I often buy puzzles for them. I don't have enough patience to work those puzzles myself, but I've learned that there's only one place for each puzzle piece to fit correctly. The same is true of this puzzle we call the church. When God puts us into the body of Christ, we fit perfectly; we look good and function effectively. If we try to force our way into the body where we wish to belong, our differences can mess up the total picture. In the right place, each disciple has an important contribution to make to the body, so God sets us in the body as it pleases him.

Writing under the inspiration of God, Paul says to the Christians at Rome that God has always had a design for his people. He had a design for Adam and Eve, but they didn't follow it. We know what happened as a result. When we do not follow the design of the church that God has created, we too fall from his favor. We create strife and dissension, hindering the work of the kingdom in destructive ways.

Why Don't We Fit?

Why, then, is it so difficult to fulfill our role in the body of Christ? Why can we not do this naturally when we get together with other believers?

One reason is human ego. The egotistical person says, "I want things my way." But remember, we are not here to get things our way; we belong to Christ, and we belong to his body. So we are not called to live our way, but his way. Our human ego has to be cleansed and sanctified to the Lord's service, just as our sins need to be forgiven. Unless egos are sanctified to the purposes of Christ, headstrong egos will overwhelm the life of the church. When people begin to make decisions out of their personal egos rather than out of a spirit of servanthood, the church suffers. When egos speak, the Holy Spirit cannot be heard. Then we have failure in the church.

A second reason we fail to fulfill our God-given role in the church is biblical illiteracy. Now I want to be kind in saying this, but clear. When God places you in the body of Christ, you are fully a member of it, but you may not be ready to function as a leader in it. You may not have matured enough spiritually to lead. In fact, you may need to be a learner for a long time. This is why Paul said to the young pastor Timothy, "Do not ordain anyone hastily" (1 Tim 5:22). If we put someone who is spiritually immature into a position of responsibility in the church, Satan will take advantage of the situation.

Sometimes we are so desperate to fill a church position that we give someone a duty for which they are ill-suited or unprepared. If someone can walk straight, we put them in charge of the ushers. But ushering is a spiritual activity, and you can make people very angry very quickly if you show poor hospitality as an usher. Singing in the choir is a spiritual activity, so is teaching a class, serving on a board, and virtually anything else we do in the life of the church. If we assign someone to a position of service before their spiritual maturity has risen to the level needed, we are going to hurt them and the entire body. Leadership must be wise enough to "govern diligently" (Rom 12:8 NIV).

Jesus Christ expects his church to bring him honor and glory, to expand the kingdom of God, and to employ effectively the spiritual gifts he has given us. But the fact is, many of our congregations are not such a pretty picture. They do not match the Bible's vision of the church because their people are biblically illiterate. Newcomers and new believers just waltz in and volunteer to do anything in the church, even to become leaders of this or that, without any significant knowledge of the Word. Yet what they know of the Bible will determine how well they serve the cause of Christ.

We behave out of our values. If our values are born out of the secular culture, we are going to behave according to secular values. If our values come out of the Bible, our behavior will come out of that. A person can be genuinely converted and have the best intentions of serving Christ but still have the wrong values. Until they have been indoctrinated in the Word of God, they are not ready to hold a position of responsibility in the church.

I have often thought that we ought to require people to take a Bible exam before serving on a church committee. Do you think that is expecting too much? Well, let me ask you this: Have you been to a medical doctor lately? Did you want a doctor who made pretty good grades in medical school, or did you care? Have you flown on an airplane lately? Did you want a pilot who had passed all the flight license exams or not? I believe the church's work is as critical as that of a medical doctor or an airplane pilot, so it requires someone who is spiritually qualified—certainly someone who knows and follows the Word of God.

When the apostles needed someone to serve tables for the church family, they said, "Friends, select from among yourselves seven men of good standing, full of the Spirit and of wisdom, whom we may appoint to this task" (Acts 6:3). They didn't choose these deacons on the basis of willingness alone. They wanted people "full of the Spirit and of wisdom" for places of service and responsibility in the church. Should we settle for anything less?

Biblical illiteracy causes more trouble in the life of the church than we may wish to admit. Suppose your congregation is looking for a pastor, so you prayerfully assemble a search committee. You ask the Lord to identify the right people to serve on this committee. You commission them for the task, saying, "We want you to pray and seek the face of God in this matter." And so they do. They eventually bring a candidate to the congregation and say, "We believe the Lord has led us to this person. So far, so good. Then what happens? "Let's all take a vote on it."

Think about it: The Lord has led your pastoral search committee to this person. They have prayed and are convinced of it. So now you're going to invite everybody in the congregation age sixteen and older who is born again to make the decision about calling your pastor? Even people who have been Christians for just a few months, even those who know virtually nothing of Scripture? Do you think the Bible supports that?

Personally, I don't think it does. I do not believe God is as likely to reveal his will in this matter to a new convert as he would to someone who is mature in the faith. Entrusting such decisions to people who know little or nothing of the Word of God is a formula for failure.

A third reason some Christians may fail to find their proper place in Christ's body is that the body itself may be too strongly influenced by its surrounding culture. The example I just gave of calling a new pastor illustrates this. Our culture has influenced our manner of conducting church business a great deal, especially when it comes to identifying our spiritual leaders. Understand that I am not opposed to the democratic method, but it is not the most biblically authentic way to make certain church decisions. Many of our decisions should be guided by more than sound business management principles and parliamentary rules, and they cannot be determined by counting votes.

We may also fail to find our proper place in the body because of the schemes and designs of the Adversary. We are engaged in spiritual warfare with Satan, and we can be sure that he does not wish the church to be victorious. He does not want the ministries of the church to succeed. He will do everything conceivable to divide and defeat the church.

However, Satan cannot do this unless we allow it. We do not have to let him prevail. We can prevent selfish egos from getting in the way of God's work. We can determine not to remain biblically illiterate. We can refuse to let secular culture dictate the way we function in the church. Let's see what the Bible says about this.

Characteristics of an Effective Church

According to Scripture, an effective church is one in which individual disciples use their spiritual gifts under the direction of the Holy Spirit. Acts 2 tells us how the early church functioned in this way. Notice the key principles of healthy church life in the following account:

> They devoted themselves to the apostles' teaching and fellowship, to the breaking of bread and the prayers. Awe came upon everyone, because many wonders and signs were being done by the apostles. All who believed were together and had all things in common; they would sell their possessions and goods and distribute the proceeds to all, as any had need. Day by day, as they spent much time together in the temple, they broke bread at home and ate their food with glad and generous hearts, praising God and having the goodwill of all the people. And day by day the Lord added to their number those who were being saved. (Acts 2:42–47)

That well describes a healthy church. Observe what these believers were doing.

First, the early Christians were learners. "They devoted themselves to the apostle's teaching." In other words, they refused to be ignorant of God's truth. They did not yet have the New Testament, so the apostles taught them precept by precept what Jesus had taught them. Many of the apostles' letters exhorted the early church to be diligent in learning these things (e.g., 2 Tim 2:15; 1 Peter 2:2; Phil 2:12). You will recall Romans 12:2, the passage we studied earlier, which emphasizes the need for God to renew our minds. One of the key characteristics of an effective church is that its people are continually learning the Word of God. They keep on reading it, discussing it, and meditating on it.

Second, they were involved in each other's lives. As the writer of Hebrews exhorted the entire church, they were "not neglecting to meet together, as is the habit of some, but encouraging one another" (10:25) This community connectivity is crucial for alignment of ministries in the congregation. In our fast-paced and separated culture, it continues to be difficult for persons within the congregation to spend quality time together. This is and will be a challenge to a relational community of believers, which the Church of God is.

Third, they demonstrated generosity toward one another and God. They shared their material resources "as any had need." Here again relational connectivity is seen in action. In order to share from resources, one needs to be aware and then willing to give. If we don't know the need or the person, most of us are hesitant to give.

Fourth, they were flexible in their methods of ministry. Acts 6:1–4 says that they realized they were not serving the needs of widows well, so they changed their ministry to respond to that need. They changed on the spot. We change, but sometimes we take too long. We need to understand what the church ought to be doing in the twenty-first century. I am not suggesting that we change the priorities of Scripture, but we must find new frameworks of ministry if we are to transform the culture of this century by being the body of Christ. If the church operates on biblical principles, we will respond to the changing needs of our world.

Are you an effective disciple in the body of Christ? Let me emphasize the word *effective*. That means you make a difference in this world, you fulfill your God-given purpose, you accomplish what God intends for you to do. If someone is sick and the physician prescribes a medication, but it makes the person no better, we say it was not effective. On the other hand, if the medication relieves the symptoms and addresses the cause of the illness, it's effective. We in the church are called to be effective servants of Christ in today's world. God has placed you in the church for that purpose. So are you doing what God has redeemed you to do, here and now?

Pause for a moment and ask that question about yourself. Here's the way I want you to frame it: If we selected ten people at random from the congregation you attend and asked this question about you, how would they answer? "Is he or she an effective disciple in the body of Christ?" What would they say?

You know, people are already asking that question about you. They observe your behavior all the time and make judgment calls on your life. (I know that's true because people call me periodically to give their judgment calls about me!) You may be the critical piece that makes the puzzle of your congregation come together. You may be the example that will cause other people to say, "Ah, I see it now! That's what it means to be a Christian." So this is a very important question: Are you an effective disciple in the body of Christ? Are you where God has placed you, living out your Christian faith in a healthy community of believers?

The Difference One Disciple Can Make

I want you to ponder this carefully, because it is the crux of the matter. What kind of picture does God see when he looks at the mosaic of your congregation? Are all of the pieces in place? Are you in place? Or are the pieces scattered, unlinked, and meaningless? Have some pieces been forced into place, or is everyone using their God-given gifts to bring the greatest glory to God?

I pray that God is able to look at you and your congregation and say, "That's my church!" God loves the church so much that he gave his Son's life for it, and he longs for us to be effective in changing the world. In order for that to happen, we must be effective disciples. We must have effective leaders. And we must minister with our leaders so that God is glorified, the church is built up, and people come to know Christ themselves.

Instead of being conformed to the world's culture, we will transform it when people see us living and working together as the body of Christ.

Chapter 7

Holy Spirit 101

There is therefore now no condemnation for those who are in Christ Jesus. For the law of the Spirit of life in Christ Jesus has set you free from the law of sin and of death. For God has done what the law, weakened by the flesh, could not do: by sending his own Son in the likeness of sinful flesh, and to deal with sin, he condemned sin in the flesh, so that the just requirement of the law might be fulfilled in us, who walk not according to the flesh but according to the Spirit. For those who live according to the flesh set their minds on the things of the flesh, but those who live according to the Spirit set their minds on the things of the Spirit. To set the mind on the flesh is death, but to set the mind on the Spirit is life and peace. —Romans 8:1–6

The church at Rome probably had some Jewish Christians as well as some Gentile Christians. Those of Jewish heritage understood what Paul meant about trying to live in conformity to the law. Judaism had 613 civil and ceremonial laws in the five books of Moses, the Torah. Jewish rabbis also made hundreds of rulings in order to help them live by those laws, rulings which were collected into the Talmud. All those laws were meant to keep them on the straight and narrow. It would be difficult to remember 613 laws, wouldn't it? So if you were a Jew in biblical times, it would be almost impossible to know if you were on the straight and narrow.

Paul tells the Christians in Rome, including the Jewish Christians, that the indwelling of the Holy Spirit is essential for the growth and maturation of a disciple of Christ. He promises that a person controlled by the Spirit is not only sure of being on the straight and narrow way but also knows true life and peace. So we might call this passage from Romans 8 the apostle Paul's course in Holy Spirit 101.

Jewish Christians knew that the Holy Spirit had come to selected individuals in Old Testament times. God sent the Spirit upon his prophets, who did miraculous and wonderful things. But the day of Pentecost revealed that the Holy Spirit is now available to everyone who serves God. So Paul tries to teach all of the Roman Christians what it means to live in the Spirit of God.

How did Paul know so much about the Holy Spirit? He was not with the other apostles on the day of Pentecost. In Paul's epistle to the Galatians, he details his conversion and the first years of his ministry for Christ. There we begin to see how he came to understand the meaning of life in the Spirit.

You will remember that he was converted on the road to Damascus and then went into the desert of Arabia for three years, where God tutored him in what he was to preach. There he received God's truth "through a revelation of Jesus Christ" (Gal 1:12). What was that truth? Let's read Paul's own summary of it:

> A person is justified not by the works of the law but through faith in Jesus Christ. And we have come to believe in Christ Jesus, so that we might be justified by faith in Christ, and not by doing the works of the law, because no one will be justified by the works of the law...through the law I died to the law, so that I might live to God. I have been crucified with Christ; and it is no longer I who live, but it is Christ who lives in me. And the life I now live in the flesh I live by faith in the Son of God, who loved me and gave himself for me. I do not nullify the grace of God; for if justification comes through the law, then Christ died for nothing. (Gal 2:16, 19–21)

He is saying that Jesus Christ came to save us while we were yet sinners. He paid the full price for our sins. He came not only to do that but to bring us hope and peace. Now the Spirit of Christ—the Holy Spirit—can live within us to control our behavior so that we do not have to rely on a massive collection of laws. This is a monumental change in the way we relate to the Lord God Almighty.

Why Neglect the Holy Spirit?

With such a marvelous promise, why have we neglected the role of the Holy Spirit in our lives? I believe this has happened for several reasons.

First, we have misunderstood the work of the Holy Spirit. We have not understood what the Holy Spirit was sent to do in each of our lives. We know that the Holy Spirit convicted us of sin before we became Christians. The Holy Spirit moved us to repentance. So we accept the fact that the Holy Spirit has been at work in us for some time. But there is much more that the Spirit can do after we become disciples of Jesus Christ. Many of us do not realize this. We are even more confused because well-known Christian leaders have told us to expect the Holy Spirit to work in sensational ways to draw attention to us.

This is the second reason some of us have neglected the role of the Holy Spirit in our lives. We have become convinced that the Holy Spirit will make a spectacle of us. We think that if we are filled by the Holy Spirit, we will begin jumping over pews or doing something else out of character. (Frankly, I am not opposed to jumping over pews, but that's not a sign that you are filled with the Holy Spirit. It's just a sign that you are physically agile.)

Third, some of us have neglected the role of the Holy Spirit because we have not based our understanding of the Spirit on the Word of God. Instead, we listen to eccentric preachers who have their own wild ideas of what the Holy Spirit ought to do.

Yet another reason we may neglect the Holy Spirit is that we mislabel or misidentify some behavior as being of the Spirit. Peer pressure or crowd hysteria may lead us to identify some pretty preposterous behavior as manifestations of the Spirit. Others may say something is a sign of God's presence and anointing, but that does not make it so.

So ponder this transforming thought: The Holy Spirit must be an intimate friend of every disciple of Jesus Christ. Only intimate daily communion with the Spirit will enable us to discern when the Spirit is truly at work in our lives, or in anyone else's.

Marks of the Spirit-Filled Life

And that's not all. Daily immersion in the Spirit of God must be accompanied by daily immersion in the Word of God. If we want to know what the work of the Spirit looks like or what a Spirit-filled life looks like, we must seek the answers in Scripture.

Paul wrote to the church at Rome that a Spirit-filled life is a temperate and controlled life (Rom 8:6). If we allow a lot of garbage into our minds, garbage will come out. Addictions begin when we expose ourselves to things that become obsessive, consuming our attention so that we no longer focus our attention upon God. When we say someone is addicted to alcohol, drugs, or pornography, what has happened? They have opened themselves just a little to something that piqued their curiosity but soon dominated their lives. An addicted person says, "I can't help myself. This thing is now in control." And they are telling the truth.

In recent years, I have become deeply concerned about what pornography is doing in the life of the church. Pornography is easily available on the Internet. With this ready availability, it gets into the minds of children, parents, and (believe it or not) their pastors. One of my good friends is Dr. Al Ells, who is a counselor to troubled pastors. As I was playing golf with Al one day, he said, "I understand you have a pornography problem."

"What?" I asked.

"You Church of God leaders have got a pornography problem. You're the general director, aren't you?"

"Yes."

"Then you've got a pornography problem, because at least 12 percent of your pastors are looking at pornography every week."

I asked where he got that statistic. He said, "I'm telling you the truth. People in ministry have a serious problem with pornography, and you need to do everything you can to stop it."

I did not want to believe him, but three weeks later I attended a ministers' meeting where three pastors stood and confessed that they were addicted to pornography. Addicted! They said it had been a long process. They started by watching just a little, then more and more, until they were viewing pornography for as much as four or five hours a day.

We monitor employees' computers at our offices to make sure they are not visiting harmful websites—i.e., sites that might be harmful to their computers or to themselves. Our employee handbook clearly states that we check all of the websites they visit. One of our ladies came to me several months ago and said, "Dr. Duncan, I didn't do anything wrong, honestly."

"What are you talking about?" I asked.

She said she had tried to order something from a website and it sent her to another site. Before she knew it, she had been redirected to another that she should not have been visiting. She knew her computer recorded this activity, so she came to me within minutes of its happening. She wanted me to know that she had not visited that salacious website intentionally.

So who's monitoring your computer? Who controls your mind? And who holds you accountable for what goes into your mind? Does the Holy Spirit control what you read, what you listen to, and who you respond to? This conscientious self-control is the first characteristic of a Spirit-filled life.

Second, the Spirit-filled life exhibits the character qualities of Christ himself. Go to Galatians 5:22–23, where the apostle Paul describes "the fruit of the Spirit." He says that if your life is directed by the Holy Spirit, these things should be evident:

The fruit of the Spirit is love, joy, peace, patience, kindness, generosity, faithfulness, gentleness, and self-control. There is no law against such things.

Remember those 613 Jewish laws? A Spirit-filled person does not violate God's law, but he is not a legalist either. He naturally does what is right because his nature has been transformed by the Spirit.

Consider each of the spiritual fruit that Paul describes. When others look at you, do they see a loving person? Is your behavior characterized by kindness, joy, patience, goodness, faithfulness,

gentleness, and self-control? Paul says those are the character qualities that typify a person who lives and walks in the Spirit of Christ.

As a specific expression of that, Paul says, "Do not let any
unwholesome talk come out of your mouths" (Eph 4:29 NIV). What
does that mean? I think it means that as a Spirit-filled person, you
do not spread gossip. You do not take the name of the Lord your
God in vain. You do not speak derogatory words to or about those
around you. Practicing such restraint is a specific manifestation of
the Holy Spirit's work in your life. Another good description of the
Spirit-filled life is found in Philippians 2:3–5a:

> Do nothing from selfish ambition or conceit, but in humility
> regard others as better than yourselves. Let each of you look
> not to your own interests, but to the interests of others. Let
> the same mind be in you that was in Christ Jesus...

That's how a sanctified believer acts. The Spirit-filled life involves
changes in our lives that are readily seen and experienced by those
around us. It means allowing the Spirit of Christ to control you seven
days a week, twenty-four hours a day, in all that you do and say.

So is the fruit of the Spirit evident in your own life? Take a
few moments for introspection. Do you have self-control, or do you
sometimes lose it? Do you get enraged at people who cut in front
of you at the grocery store or in rush-hour traffic? I used to live in
Houston, Texas, where we had a lot of road rage. An attorney there
got so angry when someone cut in front of him that he pulled out
a 9-millimeter handgun and shot out the guy's tires! You see, the
Holy Spirit changes the everyday behavior of our lives. That's not
mysterious. It's not magic. But it's clear evidence that the Holy Spirit
controls our lives.

Equipped with the Word of God

In an earlier chapter, we saw how Paul urged the church at Ephesus
to "put on the whole armor of God" (Eph 6:10–17). He says there
that Christians need to take up the sword of the Spirit, which is the
Word of God. So we return to the importance of knowing the Bible,

the inspired Word of God. We must know what's in that book. It's not sufficient to read an executive summary of it or skim through a set of CliffsNotes about it. We must commit the Word of God to our minds and hearts, because it is the weapon that the Spirit will use to guard us against evil.

So we should be in the Word every day. We should commit the Word to memory. Scripture says that the Holy Spirit will remind us of what we need to know when we come to a time of conflict (John 14:26). But for the Spirit to be able to do that, we must commit God's Word to our minds to start with.

The Lord called me into the ministry while I was in high school, and I preached my first sermon at Greenville, Tennessee. The pastor of that church said to my pastor, "We're having a baptismal service and I've got to baptize about thirty people. Could you send somebody down to deliver a mini-sermon or devotion for the occasion?" So my pastor sent me. I was fifteen years old and had never preached in my life.

"What am I going to say?" I asked.

"Come by my office on Sunday afternoon," he said, "and we'll prepare a sermon." So I stopped by his office, wrote some notes, and all the way to Greenville, I practiced that sermon. By the time I got there, I was pumped.

The church building was packed full, with at least two hundred people in attendance. The pastor introduced me, I got into that pulpit, and I started. I went through every note and read every scripture we had selected. I kept going and going, sweating and sweating. My necktie came off and I kept on going. Finally, I sat down. The sermon had lasted two minutes and thirty-two seconds.

"Thank you for that brief message, Brother Duncan," the pastor said. "We appreciate it."

Why do I tell you that story? Because it's just one example of how I have learned to live by Colossians 3:17, which says, "Whatever you do in word or deed, do all to the glory of God" (my paraphrase). I was committed that Sunday night to do my best with my inexperience. I claimed that scripture as my own very early in my Christian life and the Spirit has blessed the consequences.

Not long after that baptismal service, my pastor was going on vacation, so he asked me to visit someone in the hospital. He said, "Sister So-and-So is having major surgery and somebody ought to visit her. I'll see her before I leave town, but I'll be gone all day Saturday. I want you to go on Saturday and visit her."

So I put on my best shirt, tie, and coat. I arrived at the hospital and could not figure out what to do next. Someone in the lobby said, "May I help you, young man?"

"Yes, I'm looking for Sister So-and-So."

They said, "She's on the third floor."

I went to the third floor and got off the elevator, and there was her room. I walked back and forth in front of the room for what seemed like days. Finally, a nurse came by and said, "May I help you?"

"Yeah, I need to go in there."

"Well, then," she said, "get on in there."

The patient was stretched out with tubes and monitoring equipment everywhere. I was scared to death. I didn't know what to say, so I just stood there and didn't say a word. Not one word. I stood looking at her. I felt awful and knew that I should do something. But what? I had my pocket New Testament, so I just held it up and closed my eyes, as if to say, "Bless you."

When I couldn't stand it anymore, I turned around and left the room. I got in my car and went home, feeling like a failure. I thought, "I've blown it. I will never make it in ministry. I don't know how to do anything."

The next day, our pastor arrived late at church because he had gone to the hospital. "Ron, come in here for a minute," he said. "I want to tell you about Sister So-and-So."

"Really?"

He said, "I just left her room, and she so appreciated your silent prayer yesterday."

Then I told him the truth.

"Whatever you do in word or deed, do all to the glory of God." At the beginning of my ministry, I had so much to learn. But my meager knowledge was now controlled by Someone higher, and he used my growing knowledge of Scripture more and more effectively.

Is the Holy Spirit in control of your mind? Does your behavior emanate from the Spirit? Do the people closest to you—people whom you love and who love you—see the life of Christ in you? Do you carry the Word of God, the sword of the Spirit, in your heart and mind so that you will have it ready when you need to defend yourself against the Evil One? Do you do everything for the honor and glory of God? According to Scripture, these are the chief characteristics of a Spirit-filled life.

Chapter 8

The Power of Divine Love

Let love be genuine; hate what is evil, hold fast to what is good; love one another with mutual affection; outdo one another in showing honor. Do not lag in zeal, be ardent in spirit, serve the Lord. Rejoice in hope, be patient in suffering, persevere in prayer. Contribute to the needs of the saints; extend hospitality to strangers. Bless those who persecute you; bless and do not curse them. Rejoice with those who rejoice, weep with those who weep. Live in harmony with one another; do not be haughty, but associate with the lowly; do not claim to be wiser than you are. Do not repay anyone evil for evil, but take thought for what is noble in the sight of all. If it is possible, so far as it depends on you, live peaceably with all. Beloved, never avenge yourselves, but leave room for the wrath of God; for it is written, "Vengeance is mine, I will repay, says the Lord." No, "if your enemies are hungry, feed them; if they are thirsty, give them something to drink; for by doing this you will heap burning coals on their heads." Do not be overcome by evil, but overcome evil with good. —Romans 12:9–21

Our behavior in the body of Christ is extremely important for the growth of other individual believers. We influence the people around us by what we do, what we say, and the attitudes we display toward them. And, yes, we influence other Christian people, so our behavior will affect their spiritual health.

Remember the context of Paul's letter. He is writing to a new church in Rome that is subject to many influences. Some of these Christians have grown up in a Hebrew culture, while others have grown up in a Gentile (Greek) culture. Along the way, they learned how to survive in those respective cultures. For example, they learned that power makes right. The Roman Empire exercised a lot of military and political power over them, so they accepted the fact that they must live in subjugation to the Romans, but they also learned that powerful people can impose their wills upon weaker ones. Paul is trying to teach them something very different. He is teaching them what it means to be a Christian in a hostile environment.

Do you believe today's American culture is hostile to Christianity? Can we learn anything from Romans 12 that would help us transform our culture? Can we do it by changing our civil laws? I doubt it. We can legislate all we want, but that will not change other people's core values and behavior. Can we change our culture by force? As long as we keep criminals under the thumb of law enforcement, they may have to conform to the law. But take the thumb off, and they revert to doing whatever they wish. They haven't really changed.

The only way we are going to change our surrounding culture is to introduce a new value system to it. Spiritual formation is the development of a new value system within the individual. Culture change requires that, but it also requires developing new values within those who do not know Jesus Christ. That will happen only if they see that New Testament values can be practiced in this world. In other words, unbelieving people will not change their values until they see us change ours.

And here's the vexing part. For those of us who know Jesus Christ, changing our culture first requires us to change the value systems that we have inherited.

Values You've Been Given

It's rather like the difference between physical birth and adoption. Remember, you did not choose your mother or father; but after you were born, they may have chosen you. You did not choose the city, state or country where you were born, but you assimilated the beliefs and practices of people who lived where you were raised. If you grew up around Pittsburgh, for example, you probably became a Steelers fan. If you grew up in Chicago, you probably became a Bears fan, just by accident of location. You inherited a sports tradition based on where you were raised. So if you want to change some aspects of your tradition, you have to change some aspects of your own identity.

Paul is quite candid in telling the Roman church that this new value system he is asking them to adopt may require them to change some of their Roman traditions. The old saying goes, "When in Rome, do as the Romans do." However, Paul called the Roman Christians to live, not as their Roman neighbors lived, but as Christ taught them to live. Paul challenged them to adopt a new way of life, regardless of where they had been born and raised.

Because the Lord called us to ministry, Martha and I have lived in various places, so we have been loyal to various sports teams. We like the Cincinnati Reds. We like the Indianapolis Colts. We lived in the Houston area for fourteen years, so we even root for Houston. But Paul is talking about a much more important kind of tradition. He's talking about the value system that guides our lives. He's concerned about our spiritual formation. Although you and I may not have had much to do with traditions we assimilated in the places where life deposited us, we have everything to do with our understanding of life and our knowledge of God. We choose those things. We adopt the beliefs and practices of the new community we have chosen—the community of believers, the church.

Obstacles to Growth

If that's the case, why do we struggle with our own spiritual formation? If we love the Lord and know we belong among the Lord's people, it seems we should naturally grow within the community of faith. But that does not always happen. I think there are several reasons for this.

First, we are spiritually lazy (or, to use the word of the ancient church, slothful). Spiritual growth takes work. The Lord saves us, but that is only the beginning of our life of discipleship. Many additional choices and steps of faith must follow if we are to grow up into the character of Christ. This process is what we call spiritual development or spiritual formation.

We saw earlier how the apostle Paul went into the desert for three years after his conversion to be schooled by Jesus Christ. During that time, he began to change from the strict Jewish culture into which he had been born to the culture of the *ecclesia*, those

God had "called out" to follow Christ. He had to do that in order to become an apostle to the Gentiles. It takes just as much time for many of us to begin living the kind of life God expects of his children. But if we are lazy, the process of spiritual formation can take much longer.

A second reason our spiritual formation may be delayed is the fact that we are reluctant to confront our archaic traditions. In the early decades of the Church of God, for example, we observed many prohibitions to demonstrate that we were not a part of the world. Our men did not wear neckties and our ladies did not wear feathers in their hats or rouge on their cheeks. No one wore rings, not even wedding bands, because the world did that and we had been set apart from the world. By stripping off these outward adornments, we tried to say to our secular society, "We are different." As time passed, that began to change. We recognized that a transformed life was best demonstrated, not by what we wore, but by what we believed and how we treated others. The clothing prohibitions went away because a higher standard was introduced.

Paul illustrates this in the Bible text we read at the beginning of this chapter. The Bible's standards may be at odds with traditions we have observed for many years, so it's difficult to turn from our ways to God's way. Yet that's part of our spiritual formation.

Third, we may have trouble with spiritual formation because we like our current lifestyle too much. But if we are to grow spiritually, we cannot be satisfied to remain as we are for the rest of our lives.

A fourth reason we may struggle with spiritual formation is that we feel pressure from our peers. We fear they will make fun of us because we are changing. So we have to choose between our peers' expectations and Christ's.

Are You a Spiritual Asset or Liability?

The transforming truth from this scripture is this: Your behavior and mine is either an asset or a liability to the body of Christ. It's not neutral. We either strengthen the faith of other believers or we weaken it. What will determine whether we are assets to the body of Christ, rather than liabilities, as we move through the long process of our own spiritual growth?

First, according to the apostle Paul, it depends on the quality of our love. "Let love be genuine," he says (v 9). Other people can tell the difference between an attitude of tolerance and an attitude of genuine love. They know when they are not being loved. So Paul challenges the Christians at Rome, and subsequently us, to exhibit an extraordinary kind of love toward one another. Jesus told the Twelve about this agape love when he said, "I give you a new commandment, that you love one another. Just as I have loved you, you also should love one another" (John 13:34). He challenged them to move from brotherly love to agape love, the kind of love Jesus himself had for others. This unlimited love comes from the Father. So for us to become the kind of disciples who honor the Father and his Son, who contribute to the health of the body of Christ, we need to look critically at the quality of our love.

Martha and I have been privileged to be married for forty-six years. (She deserves a lot of the credit for that!) But I can tell you that if we still had the quality of love we had at age fifteen, our marriage would have failed. At fifteen, we were just infatuated teenagers. We didn't really understand the depths of genuine love. We did not know how the experiences of life would test our love. So the quality of our love had to grow over the years in order for our relationship to thrive.

Similarly, there is a discernable difference in the quality of people's love. Paul says Christian disciples should have "genuine" love for one another. We ought to be devoted to one another. This high-quality love is not short-lived. It just grows and grows and grows as time goes on.

The love that you had for the Lord Jesus Christ when you were first converted was wonderful, but it will not sustain you throughout your life. It must grow. Your love for other believers must grow more mature as well. This is why Paul says, "Let love be genuine."

Second, our contribution to church life depends on our spiritual fervor. Often, old-timers will say that new converts are "on fire for the Lord." Then, two or three years later, they ask, "What happened to the fire?" It's easy to let our spiritual fervor wane.

Fervor comes from setting the right priorities in our lives. What priority do the things of God have in your life? Kingdom matters must have top priority for you or your spiritual fervor will cool.

Jeff Saturday, who was the center for the Indianapolis Colts, is a fine Christian man. He was a guest speaker for a meeting that Martha and I attended recently, and we sat right next to him. Here is a pro athlete who makes millions of dollars and has become a celebrity worldwide, yet he and his wife told us about the priority of Jesus Christ in their family.

Every morning, as they have breakfast with their kids, they share family devotions. Jeff asks the children, "What are you going to do for the Lord today?" You see, he makes Christ a priority in those children's minds.

Then Jeff goes to work and enters the locker room to suit up. An NFL locker room is not exactly a cathedral; all sorts of ungodly stuff goes on, and all sorts of profane language is used. But Jeff and several of his teammates huddle together in the locker room to pray and share their Christian witness. Their fervor comes from maintaining the right priorities in life.

Does the Lord have that kind of priority in your life? You see, spiritual formation is not just a one-time thing; it's not a course of study that you take just after you become a Christian. Spiritual formation is a consistent movement toward the goal that God has set for you. So the apostle Paul says in verse 11, "Do not lag in zeal, be ardent in spirit, serve the Lord." You do that by beginning every day with God.

Third, our contribution to the life of other believers will depend on having healthy attitudes for life. Look at what Paul says in verse 12: "Rejoice in hope, be patient in suffering, persevere in prayer." He is talking about our attitudes.

Attitude influences the way we think and behave. I visit many congregations every year, and some are so lethargic they seem "as dead as four o'clock." The people are tired and feel that the whole world is against them. They are weary of living. An evangelist can preach and preach and preach to people like that, but they will not change until their attitude toward life changes. A healthy attitude says, "Lord, whatever comes my way, I know you have allowed it to come. So I am ready for it." Remember what Paul wrote to the church in Corinth:

> No testing has overtaken you that is not common to everyone. God is faithful, and he will not let you be tested beyond your strength, but with the testing he will also provide the way out so that you may be able to endure it. (1 Cor 10:13)

Fourth, our healthy contribution to the life of the church body depends on having Christ-honoring relationships within the body. "Bless those who persecute you; bless and do not curse them. Rejoice with those who rejoice, weep with those who weep. Live in harmony with one another," Paul writes.

One thing we started doing at our congregation in Pasadena, Texas, was aimed at building such relationships. When another congregation did something outstanding in our community, we sent a note of congratulations to them and bought flowers for their worship service the next Sunday. Some asked, "Why are you doing this?" We did it because the scripture says, "Rejoice with those who rejoice" (Rom 12:15). We Church of God folks say we reach our hands in fellowship to every blood-washed one. So we ought to rejoice, not only with Church of God folks, but with all of God's folks. When God does something wonderful through other Christians in your community, share their joy.

On the other hand, when a church is going through a difficult time, call someone there and say, "I want you to know that we're lifting you up in prayer." People may scratch their heads and ask, "What kind of people are these?" We're the kind of people who take the New Testament seriously.

Verse 16 says more about attitudes that are conducive to spiritual growth: "Live in harmony with one another; do not be haughty, but associate with the lowly; do not claim to be wiser than you are." Verse 18 says, "If it is possible, so far as it depends on you, live peaceably with all." Such action steps emerge out of a genuine love for other Christians.

Do the Right Thing—Regardless!

Fifth, we will build the faith of other believers in the body of Christ if we do the right thing, regardless of the cost. That's what Paul says: "Do not repay anyone evil for evil, but take thought for what is noble in the sight of all" (v 17).

My father had a home improvement business as I was growing up. That business often tested his integrity and confronted him with the necessity of doing the right thing. He never signed a contract with anybody but shook hands with everybody. That's the way he did business, and it's one of the great lessons my father gave me. His word was his bond.

Once, a certain lady bought a storm door from us, so Dad dispatched my brother to install it. My brother came back and said, "We have a problem. That house is crooked."

"The house is crooked?" Dad asked.

"Yeah," my brother said. "It's cockeyed."

"Well, how did you hang the door?"

"I squared the door, but it looks funny," my brother said.

In about five minutes, this lady called my Dad, very upset. "Your son put my door up crooked."

"Well, he told me that the house is a little out of square," Dad said. "So it may look wrong, but the door is square."

"No, it's not."

Dad got in his truck and drove over there with a carpenter's level. He showed her that the door was indeed level and square. "It still doesn't look right," she said. "I want it changed."

Dad called my brother and said, "Come back over here and change the door."

How do you "fix" a square door? You hang it crooked so it will match the crooked house. So my brother went back for a second time and changed the door. It would still open, but it matched the tilt of the house.

The lady called again to say, "This door doesn't look right. It's still crooked."

"We know it's crooked," Dad replied. "Your house is crooked, and you wanted the door to match it."

"That's no good," she said. "Come back and fix it."

Dad sent my brother back for a third attempt. My brother was about seventeen at the time and was getting frustrated, fiddling with this door. So he said to the lady, "I want you to watch while I put this door up."

She came outside and watched as he put in shims to tilt the door frame one way or the other. "Now you tell me when it looks good to you. That's where I'll put the screw," he said.

They hung the door according to the customer's eye. It wasn't square, but our customer was happy. Most business owners would have said, "Ma'am, we put up your door properly and it's square. If you want to change it, good luck. See you later." Not Dad. He determined to do the right thing, regardless of the cost to him.

That illustration may seem comical to you, but it has an important lesson for our dealings with each other in the church. What if you have to do the right thing for somebody who has talked against you? What if you have to do the right thing for somebody who has unfairly criticized you? What if you know you are in the right, but you have offended your brother or sister? These are the dilemmas Paul is raising for the Christians in Rome. He says we must do the right thing, regardless of the cost to ourselves. That's the only way we can make a difference in our world. It requires us to have a completely different value system from the world's.

Next, Paul tells us to deal redemptively with our conflicts. "Beloved, never avenge yourselves...Do not be overcome by evil, but overcome evil with good" (vv 19, 21). Is this how you deal with conflicts in your congregation? You see, the way the church handles its personal disputes will reveal the values we have.

What do you need to work on in your own spiritual formation? In what respect do you need to grow so that your culture can see that you are a disciple of Jesus Christ? Do you live like everyone else around you, or do you live like Christ? I long for the day when every church in America reflects New Testament values. When that day comes, there will be a mighty reformation. But it will not come until we, the people of God, get serious about living according to the standards of God.

Chapter 9

Accountable for Spiritual Growth

We do not live to ourselves, and we do not die to ourselves. If we live, we live to the Lord, and if we die, we die to the Lord; so then, whether we live or whether we die, we are the Lord's...each of us will be accountable to God. —Romans 14:7–8, 12

Our behavior as Christians has both earthly and eternal consequences. This is why the apostle Paul devotes so much of his epistle to the Romans (three chapters, Rom 13–15) to the theme of accountability. As he nears the end of this substantive letter to the Roman Christians, he wants them to understand fully that their lifestyle and behavior do matter and will be judged by God.

That statement may puzzle you. After all, as a Christian you know you have been saved from eternal condemnation for your sins. You no longer have to worry about eternal damnation in hell. So why does Paul raise for you the prospect of God's judgment? Because your behavior, from the day of your conversion until the day of your physical death, is still subject to God's judgment. We Christians cannot do as we please; we are called to live a faithful, holy life. On the last day, we shall stand before God to give an account of whether we have done so.

We have relatively few scriptures about judgment day in the New Testament, but we ought to study closely those we do have. For example, consider the great white throne judgment described by John the apostle, writing from the Isle of Patmos about forty years after Paul wrote his epistle to the Romans:

Then I saw a great white throne and the one who sat on it; the earth and the heaven fled from his presence, and no place was found for them. And I saw the dead, great and small, standing before the throne, and books were opened. Also another book was opened, the book of life. And the dead were judged according to their works, as recorded in the books. And the sea gave up the dead that were in it, Death and Hades gave up the dead that were in them, and all were judged according to what they had done. Then Death and Hades were thrown into the lake of fire. This is the second death, the lake of fire; and anyone whose name was not found written in the book of life was thrown into the lake of fire. (Rev 20:11–15)

Both Paul and John say we are going to give an account to God for the way we live our faith. Now consider this judgment day prophecy that Jesus gives us in Matthew 25:

"When the Son of Man comes in his glory, and all the angels with him, then he will sit on the throne of his glory. All the nations will be gathered before him, and he will separate people one from another as a shepherd separates the sheep from the goats, and he will put the sheep at his right hand and the goats at the left. Then the king will say to those at his right hand, 'Come, you that are blessed by my Father, inherit the kingdom prepared for you from the foundation of the world; for I was hungry and you gave me food, I was thirsty and you gave me something to drink, I was a stranger and you welcomed me, I was naked and you gave me clothing, I was sick and you took care of me, I was in prison and you visited me.' Then the righteous will answer him, 'Lord, when was it that we saw you hungry and gave you food, or thirsty and gave you something to drink? And when was it that we saw you a stranger and welcomed you, or naked and gave you clothing? And when was it that we saw you sick or in prison and visited you?' And the king will answer them, 'Truly I tell you, just as you did it to one of the least of these who are members of my family, you did it to me.' Then he will say to those at his left hand, "You that are accursed, depart from me into the eternal fire prepared for the devil and his angels; for I was hungry and you gave me no food, I was thirsty and you gave me nothing to drink, I was a stranger and you did not welcome me, naked and you did not give me clothing, sick and in prison and you did not visit me.' Then they also will answer, 'Lord, when was it that we saw you hungry or thirsty or a stranger or naked or sick or in prison, and did not take care of you?' Then he will answer them, 'Truly I tell you, just as you did not do it to one of the least of these, you did not do it to me.' And these will go away into eternal punishment, but the righteous into eternal life." (Matt 25:31–46)

We need to practice spiritual discipline because our activities will be subject to eternal judgment.

Yet some believers try to avoid thinking about this. They don't want to believe there will be a judgment day. "How can a loving God hold us accountable?" they ask. Yet it is clearly foretold by the Bible. Whether we believe it or not doesn't change the reality.

Some are deceived by the Adversary into rationalizing their ungodly behavior. "Those church people are just too narrow," the Enemy says. "It's okay to be belligerent. It's okay to lie. It's okay not to care." No, it isn't. We will give an account to God for every word, every deed, and every thought of our lives.

Some say, "I don't need to read this. I have too many other things to worry about." But when the Bible speaks into our lives, we are accountable for it. "Anyone, then, who knows the right thing to do and fails to do it, commits sin" (James 4:17). We are not talking about the sin of Adam. We're talking about your sin and mine—the things we intentionally choose to do, which disappoint our heavenly Father. We are accountable for all of these things.

Some Christians believe that once they are saved, they can live any way they wish. That's not what the Bible says. Scripture says that

Satan cannot pluck you out of God's hand (John 10:28–29), but you can jump out because you have free will. As long as you have free will, you are accountable for what you do with it.

A life of holiness means we exercise self-control according to the Word of God so that we live in ways that honor God the Father and his Son Jesus Christ. Paul addresses numerous areas of personal behavior in his letter to the Romans. Most likely, it was written on his third missionary journey about AD 57. A few years earlier, in AD 49, Emperor Claudius had expelled all Jews from Rome. When Paul writes this letter, however, the Jews have returned. Jewish Christians are again present in the congregation, so Paul addresses several direct appeals to them. The Jewish and Gentile Christians had a dispute: the Jews believed they should not eat certain foods and the Gentile Christians resented having these rules imposed upon church life. Paul was aware of this dispute, so he gives some instructions about how these Christians can live together in unity.

In essence, he says, "Listen, friends. You will have to give an account to God for your behavior, so stop these squabbles. The church does not exist to please you but to please God." Paul urges them to stop judging each other and accept one another in Christ. Let's look briefly at the specific instructions concerning Christian unity that he gives in Romans 13–15.

Foundations of Christian Unity

In chapter 13, he says that Christians should submit themselves to their governing authorities. The Jewish and Gentile Christians had different points of view about the Roman civil authority, so Paul tried to give them a Christian point of view. He says no one is in a position of authority unless God has put them there. "Pay to all what is due them—taxes to whom taxes are due, revenue to whom revenue is due, respect to whom respect is due, honor to whom honor is due" (Rom 13:7). The Christian principle is, honor and respect those who are in positions of authority over you.

We American Christians have a tough time with this principle, but I am not going to debate its merits here. I encourage you to study this passage prayerfully and see what it means to you. Find out what

Scripture says about the appropriate Christian response toward those in authority, whether you agree with them or not. Not only is this essential to civic peace, but it's essential to unity within the church.

The second foundation of Christian unity, according to Paul, is maintaining our morality at the highest levels. In the city of Rome at that time, you could have anything you wanted. Immorality was accepted and openly practiced in the streets. Paul said to his Christian friends, "Ungodliness may be all around you, but you must maintain the highest moral standard of conduct." If only that were true of Christians today! Our morals do not need to be lowered to achieve unity, but raised to God's standard. Paul exhorts us to "put on the Lord Jesus Christ, and make no provision for the flesh, to gratify its desires" (Rom 13:14).

In chapter 14, Paul says we also build Christian unity if we accept those whose faith is weak. He talks about the controversy over eating meat, the appropriate times for public worship, and so on. He points out that Christians are at different places in their faith development, but they still serve the same Lord.

Do this experiment with me: In your mind, draw an imaginary circle. Now draw another circle outside that one. In geometry, these would be called concentric circles. The contents of the outer circle are an equal distance from the inner circle, the core. Imagine that the inner circle represents Jesus Christ, while the outer circle represents all of us who follow Christ. We find many differences among the people in the outer circle—differences of nationality, differences in food preference, differences in education, and so on. Yet we are all equally close to Jesus Christ. This is a picture of the church. We have unity because we have a common Lord who is at the center of our lives and who accepts all of us equally.

My first pastor was in his twenties when he accepted the pastorate of our church, and I felt he was an outstanding preacher. The previous pastor was sixty-five, and I did not know him very well. Was either of them closer to Jesus because one was familiar to me and the other was not? No. Was either of them closer to Jesus because one was a gifted preacher and the other might not have been? No. You get the picture. Paul says we need to accept and respect one another despite our differences. Strong Christians should encourage and honor weak Christians, and vice versa, because we all serve Jesus Christ.

My brother is five years older than I am. We disagree on Scripture now and then, but he's still my brother and a fellow believer, so I know he is going to heaven. (He'll find out he's wrong when he gets there. We joke about that.) You see, our interpretations about certain biblical texts do not matter as much as our relationship with the Lord. What matters eternally is that our hearts are right and we are living holy lives. We are at different places in our faith development, but that should not disrupt our fellowship either. Paul would say that our unity does not depend on our being in complete agreement or in lock step with each other on our spiritual journey.

Unity Essential to God's Work

You see, Paul was preparing the church in Rome for a tremendous expansion of the kingdom of God. The church had to understand its nature as a community of diverse people. The thing that bound them together was their faith in Jesus Christ. That should have been enough to enable them to go forward. Sadly, some of them had established other criteria that separated them and kept them from being the kind of people God had called them to be. This is why Paul reminded them of their ultimate accountability before God. Because God was their judge, the Roman Christians did not have to measure up to one another's standards. Gentile Christians and Jewish Christians could worship and work together to accomplish mighty things for God in Rome.

Where is God trying to get you together with other Christians to do a mighty work? You see, that Great Commission never goes away. We are to go and make disciples where we live and in the entire world. We will not make disciples for Christ if we cannot get our act together as his body. Are there standards of behavior in the body? Absolutely. But we have to use wisdom in applying those standards so that we do not get sidetracked from the central mission Christ has given us.

Five Great Truths of Romans

The book of Romans has five overarching truths that we should summarize here. Romans has often been described as the epistle of grace, but when we see the book in its entirety, we realize it is also an epistle of accountability.

The first truth is, *we are saved by grace.* "God demonstrates his own love for us in this: While we were still sinners, Christ died for us" (Rom 5:8 NIV). Many of us have used a set of Scripture texts called "the Roman road" to lead people to the Lord. That's the beginning verse of the road. None of us can save ourselves from the consequences of sin. Each of us must be saved by grace through the atoning sacrifice of Jesus Christ.

Second, *God Almighty has placed every believer in the body of Christ, the church.* It is essential for us to grasp this fact. If you are a born-again person, you belong somewhere in the church. There are no free-agent Christians; they don't exist. If you belong to the Lord, you need to be involved in a local congregation, because you are a member of Christ's body.

Third, *every believer has a specific role in the church, which is determined by the Holy Spirit.* The Holy Spirit sets us in the church as he wills. Our assignments are not ranked in any sort of hierarchy; they're just different from one another. Every believer is an essential piece of the puzzle that is the church. Whatever role God has given you, rejoice and be glad in it.

When I was a pastor in Mansfield, Ohio, we had a "singing Christmas tree" about thirty-five feet high outside the church building. Choir members would take their places in the Christmas tree to sing while we narrated the Christmas story to visitors who drove by. Putting up the tree took a lot of volunteers, and an eight-year-old boy wanted to help. Those timbers were so heavy that he couldn't lift them, so other volunteers said, "Come on, Johnny, get out of the way. We need to get this done."

I felt sorry for him, so I said, "Johnny, I have an important job for you."

"What, pastor?"

"I want you to be the door holder."

"What's that?" he asked.

"Come on, I'll show you." As volunteers brought the tree's components from storage in a nearby house that we owned, the door slammed shut and they would run into it. I said, "Johnny, when they come out, your job is to hold the door so they don't tear it up. That way, they can get the Christmas tree out."

That little boy was so happy. He told all of his friends at Sunday school, "Guess what? I was the door holder!" You know, God needs a lot of door holders in his kingdom.

Fourth, *every believer is called to live a gospel lifestyle.* That's the holy life we examined in the previous chapter.

Finally, *each of us must give a personal account to God.* Are you ready to give an account for your life? Your words? Your actions? Your attitudes? If the answer is no, I invite you to come back to the throne of grace and say, "Father, I have missed the mark. I tried my best, but I've fallen short. Please forgive me. If I leave this earth tonight, I want to be able to stand before you and know that I've been forgiven."

Yes, there is accountability at the throne of God—and there is forgiveness.

Chapter 10

Hope for the Future

Now to God who is able to strengthen you according to my gospel and the proclamation of Jesus Christ, according to the revelation of the mystery that was kept secret for long ages but is now disclosed, and through the prophetic writings is made known to all the Gentiles, according to the command of the eternal God, to bring about the obedience of faith—to the only wise God, through Jesus Christ, to whom be the glory forever! Amen. —Romans 16:25–27

In previous chapters, we saw how the apostle Paul explained to the Roman Christians the relationship between God's grace and our accountability in a life of Christian discipleship. He says that Christians are to love each other as Christ loves them and that when this love is evident, we will be transformed by the renewing of our minds. As we begin to be transformed spiritually, the Word of God takes root in our lives. The Word becomes our source of unwavering faith. As we deal with life's difficult issues, we can apply what we've learned of the Word to those difficult questions.

Paul further says that every Christian has a role in the body of Christ because God places us in his church. The Holy Spirit gives us direction and teaches us the truth, just as Jesus promised the Twelve. And God expects us to grow in our spiritual formation because, at some point, we must give an account to him. All of these truths are foundational to understanding the overall life and dynamics of the church.

In this passage from Romans 16, we see that the church is God's most powerful tool for bringing about transformation in the world's culture. That is why, although the church has had difficult times and incredible struggles, it has always survived. It is the church of the living God. How vibrant and how dynamic a local congregation is depends on the individuals within it. But even though we see some weak and lethargic congregations, let us always remember that the universal church is God's mighty army for redemptive change.

If your local church is not dynamic and vibrantly alive, you ought to find out why—and start the assessment with yourself. Don't point your finger at someone else. Ask yourself what kind of changes should occur in your personal life in order for the church to be strong. That's what Paul asked the Christians at Rome to do. He challenged them at this crucial time in history and in this strategic city to be the kind of church that would infiltrate Roman imperial culture and spread the gospel through it.

The church in Rome had a difficult task. Yes, they had the apostles visiting them. They had testimonies of eyewitnesses to Jesus' ministry. They probably had letters of encouragement from other churches in the empire. And they had the Holy Spirit. But they still had an overwhelming assignment: Change the world.

If we go back to the book of Acts, we find that the assignment started with just a few disciples gathered in an upper room. It spread from 12 disciples to 70, from 70 to 120, and from 120 to 3,000. Then it just began to explode.

Sounds like the early church was quite effective, so what were their problems? They lacked training. They lacked material resources. They lacked a unified vision of how Christians should grow spiritually. (If you became a Christian, did you have to be circumcised? Did you have to follow the 613 rules of the Torah? They did not agree on these questions.) They lacked a history, so they lacked practical experience of dealing with cultural problems. At the same time, they had a hostile government. And yet they survived and thrived. Why?

Secrets of a Thriving Church

Romans 16:3–15 gives us important clues. Look at the co-workers in the kingdom that Paul lists in the Romans 16 passage. He says, "Greet Aquila and Priscilla," and many others. Paul says that folks like these, committed to the work of Christ, were at the core of church life. They were one of the key reasons the church survived.

A second reason was that the Christians confronted untruth in their midst (see Rom 16:16–19). If you tolerate falsehood in your congregation, you cannot expect to survive. True, confrontation can be messy, but it's necessary. In 1 Corinthians 3, for example, Paul confronts the church in Corinth about several things that were causing division among them. "You are still of the flesh," he says. "For as long as there is jealousy and quarreling among you, are you not of the flesh, and behaving according to human inclinations?" (v 3). You see, when Christ comes into your life, you are changed. You are turned around. That's what the word *repentance* means. You exchange your worldly value system for that of Christ. And since your value system determines your behavior, if your behavior is still ungodly, your value system hasn't changed. Paul said to the church of his day and to us, "Your value system must reflect the Word of God."

I taught some college courses for a while and one assignment I routinely gave was this: "Take your life and match it up with Scripture. Identify ten typical behaviors in your life and see if they match up with Scripture." Students didn't like that assignment. They much preferred a test that required fill-in-the-blank or multiple-choice answers, not one that required them to look at the whole Bible. But that's exactly what Paul is challenging us to do. The parable of the sower in Matthew 13 is significant in this context:

> That same day Jesus went out of the house and sat beside the sea. Such great crowds gathered around him that he got into a boat and sat there, while the whole crowd stood on the beach. And he told them many things in parables, saying: "Listen! A sower went out to sow. And as he sowed, some seeds fell on the path, and the birds came and ate them up. Other seeds fell on rocky ground, where they did not have much soil, and they sprang up quickly, since they had no depth of soil. But when the sun rose, they were scorched; and since they had no root, they withered away. Other seeds fell among thorns, and the thorns grew up and choked them. Other seeds fell on good soil and brought forth grain, some

a hundredfold, some sixty, some thirty. Let anyone with ears listen!" (Matt 13:1–9)

According to this parable, the seed of God's truth that falls into your life has a one-in-four chance of bearing fruit. Just one in four! That's a sobering thought. It means you have to decide, "Am I going to let the Word make a difference in the way I live?" In order for that to happen, you must nourish and protect it, and root out everything that attempts to crowd it out. The early Christians knew this, and they survived because they confronted untruth in their midst.

Third, they survived because they knew they had the power to crush Satan. Paul told his friends at Rome, "The God of peace will shortly crush Satan under your feet" (Rom 16:20a). Now do you fear Satan? Do you fear your Adversary? A basic principle we learned in the United States Army was, understand your enemy. Soldiers cannot prevail in battle unless they understand their enemies. They ask themselves, "What weapons does the enemy have? What strength do we need to overcome the enemy? What tactics will we use to do that?" The same thing is true in the life of the church. The church is always under assault by the Enemy. So many adverse things going on in the life of individual believers and in the church as a whole are actually caused by the Enemy.

Church leaders have a primary responsibility to deal with the Enemy, because the Enemy wishes to devour, disrupt, and destroy what God has planted. What does it take to overcome the Enemy? This is why we have God's Word, the sword of the Lord. The Word will help us confront, deflect, and defend ourselves and the church against Satan's assaults. We must be strong, stand firm, and aggressively pursue our Enemy with the weapon God has placed in our hands.

Fourth, the early church survived and thrived because they knew they had a mandate from Almighty God. Think about the most important letter you've ever received. When I was a young man, I knew I might receive a letter telling me to report for military duty. That was a pretty important letter. When I applied for admission to college and waited to get an acceptance letter, that was an important piece of correspondence. But the letter that came to these Christians in Rome was from Almighty God, the Creator of the universe. Paul wrote it under the inspiration of the Holy Spirit, so it originated with God himself. And its mandate could be summed up in one sentence: "Church, be about my divine business." This mandate was one reason they survived. No matter what trials and persecutions came their way, the early Christians knew they were on assignment from God.

The Promise of His Spirit

How were they able to fulfill this supernatural assignment? How can we? How did God equip the church in Rome—and us—to carry the gospel of his Son Jesus Christ to all nations of the world?

Notice what is promised to us in the New Testament: Jesus said, "I will ask the Father, and he will give you another Advocate, to be with you forever. This is the Spirit of truth, whom the world cannot receive, because it neither sees him nor knows him. You know him, because he abides with you, and he will be in you" (John 14:16–17). The New Testament Greek word that is translated as "Advocate" is *paracletos*, which means "someone who stands beside you." If you are summoned to court to face an accusation in front of a judge, an advocate is someone who says, "You're not alone. I'm standing here with you, answering on your behalf." Jesus said that the Holy Spirit will be our Advocate when we face the most difficult tests of our assignment.

Some years ago, I received a telephone call from a mother who said, "My daughter is possessed. She is screaming and carrying on. Pastor, can you come over?" So I went. I had not encountered this kind of situation before. As I came to the door of the house, I heard loud screaming inside. I knocked and the mother came to the door in tears. She looked like she'd had no sleep the night before and was completely disheveled. She said, "Can you do something to help us?"

Her sixteen-year-old daughter was jumping around, doing all sorts of crazy antics, and when I entered the room she didn't stop. She just got more agitated. So I prayed out loud, "In the name of Jesus Christ by the power of the Holy Spirit, I rebuke what is going on. I rebuke it in the name of Christ!"

That continued for thirty minutes or so—I kept on rebuking and the girl kept on jumping around. Finally, she went limp and fell quiet. Her mother was thrilled. I was exhausted, and I knew I'd been up against something that was not of this world. Only by the power of Almighty God did this possessed girl become quiet.

The mother later told me that this girl was a drug addict, so who knows what was going on in her head. We got her some mental-health care and separated her from those who were leading her down this road. Looking back on that experience, I know her deliverance was accomplished by the power of Almighty God. That girl was helped and the Enemy was defeated by the power of God.

We have the Holy Spirit within us, so we need to act victoriously. We need not fear what the Enemy may throw at us.

Dr. Jeffrey Frymire is a hefty guy about six foot three inches tall who served on the search committee that called me to Church of God Ministries. Throughout that process, he often said, "Dr. Duncan, I've got your back." It was reassuring to know that this strong brother would stand beside me, come what may.

Who has your back? Do you live in the knowledge that the Holy Spirit has his arm of advocacy around you? Are you living in full confidence of the presence of God? Remember that when you have the Holy Spirit dwelling within, you can call upon Scripture, the sword of the Holy Spirit, to strengthen and protect you.

In our office building at Anderson, we have an upstairs room full of canes, wheelchairs, and crutches that were discarded when people were healed during camp meetings years ago. That room is a reminder of those who have gone before us who withstood the tests of the Enemy and went on to make a difference in this world. That's a great heritage. What heritage of faith will you leave to the next generation?

Praying and Fasting

Yes, we have resources that the church in Rome didn't have. With these resources, the only way we can fail to carry out the mandate of God is through a lack of prayer and fasting. In 2011, Church of God Ministries launched a ministry emphasis for the forty days leading up to Easter that we called Focus 40. We had 711 congregations from eleven countries participate in that effort. We heard phenomenal stories about what happened during that season of prayer, fasting, and seeking God's face.

In 2012, the second Focus 40 emphasis was directed at reaching the lost in our local communities. We prayed for twenty-five thousand conversions to Christ during those forty days. That was a big goal. How could it possibly be achieved? Jesus said that some things can only be accomplished through prayer and fasting (Mark 9:28–29), and we believed this would be one of them. Prayer is essential to our life and ministry.

As you read the Gospels, notice how many times Jesus withdrew from the crowds and from his own disciples to pray. He was the Son of God, but he was also fully human. Like us, he needed to set aside times when God could speak to him without distraction, to give him the encouragement and guidance he needed. Especially in difficult times, Jesus prayed alone. So must we. We have such wonderful resources for ministry, yet we must take time to commune with our Lord or we will not accomplish what he has given us to do.

If we commit ourselves fully to God, I believe he will use us to turn the world upside down (see Acts 17:1–6). Individuals called by God and placed in the church by his Holy Spirit can accomplish a major transformation of the culture. He did it in the first century, and he can do it again today.

A Final Word

What effect has the expounded Scripture made in your life? Maybe you are living as you ought in full harmony with Scripture and the leading of the Holy Spirit. If that is not the case, what is keeping you from experiencing the fullness of God's grace and the joy of a fulfilled life?

When we are in harmony with Scripture and the Holy Spirit, we have a perspective, an outlook, and experience that is beyond comprehension (Eph 3:20). My desire is for all persons to know Jesus Christ in such a relational way so as to bring divine wholeness to everyday living. Allow the Word of God to penetrate your mind and heart and then witness the marvelous results.